W9-BQY-523

First published on cassette tape and in note form, 1977
Second publishing in booklet form, 1990
by *Heritage Institute Ministries*

First printing, 1993
Second printing, 1995
Third printing, 1995
Fourth printing, 1997
Fifth printing, 2001

Published by the *Plymouth Rock Foundation*
1120 Long Pond Road, Plymouth, Massachusetts 02360

Printed in the USA by Automated Graphic Systems, White Plains, MD

ISBN 0-942516-14-1

TABLE OF CONTENTS

Introduction

IT IS TIME FOR CHRISTIANS TO WAKE UP AND PLAN AHEAD FOR THE NEXT GENERATION

Across America and around the world we have become experts at identifying the evils of our day. We lament the high rate of divorce, abortion, and the number of teens who are practicing fornication and yet wishing at the same time to be released from its consequences. We live in a society that is more concerned with treating symptoms than their causes. This book is designed to declare a trumpet call for such a time as this.

When we are intoxicated with detecting symptoms, repeating slogans, pet phrases and quick fixes, it is time the root of the problem is revealed and dealt with clearly. Not that this is a pioneer effort. Much has been gleaned by those from whom I have studied prior to 1976 when a way was being paved in the 20th century wilderness of premarital preparation and counseling. To my delight, the number of other books and calls to true purity that have arisen since 1976 when I first put my pen to paper on this topic has been refreshing.

It is time for believers to recognize that most of the weeds that choke off the fruit in the teen years was grown by the adult generation. We choose the battles we will fight when our children are young. If we ignore the area of passion, we will fight a war of lust that comes from our own making years later. My intent when initially writing this book was to blend together the following key ingredients for parents and teens to regain the foresight necessary to see another generation of purity arise in the land.

Love Fulfills the Law

> *"Love worketh no ill to his neighbor; therefore love is the fulfilling of the law."* - Romans 13:10

Dating is rooted in a deceptive practice of working ill upon one's neighbor. We defraud one another but claim to do it in the love of Christ. We have yet to learn about true love, yet only true love *fulfills* the Law. We don't even know what God's Law requires anymore, so we have no idea when we are truly loving or whether we practice a counterfeit. Christians need to wake up and clearly discern whether or not we are moving in the power of His Love that is freely given to us by the grace of Jesus Christ.

Awake Out of our Sleep

> *"And that, knowing the time, that now it is high time to awake out*
> *of sleep: for now is our salvation nearer than when we believed. The night is far spent, the day is at hand; let us therefore cast off the works of darkness and put on the armor of light."*
> - Romans 13:11-12

It is time to awake out of our sleep of slothfulness in regard to laying a foundation for marriage. We are closer now to the Second Coming of Christ. As God's providential plan moves on to completion, it is more urgent that we move with Him and not against Him. The night of frivolity, fornication and slothfulness has been far spent. We no longer save in order to invest in the future, spending passion much the way we have squandered our money. As a result, we live in debt, unable to pour true love into our present marriages, never mind the future ones.

It is time indeed to cast off the works of darkness, and put on the armor of light. Let us not deceive ourselves into constantly thinking that things just turn out fine for no reason at all. What we see are the effects of what we have sown and practiced. I write this book to define both the darkness that must be removed and the armor that must be worn in order to build the foundations.

Walk in Foresight

> *"Let us walk honestly, as in the day, not in rioting and drunkenness, not in chambering and wantonness, not in strife and envying. But put ye on the Lord Jesus Christ, and make not provision for the flesh, to fulfill the lusts thereof."*
> - Romans 13:13-14

Finally, it is time to walk honestly (or *decently*) rather than be an embarrassment to our Lord and the Christian faith. What Christians often practice the least is *foresight*. This verse makes this clear: we must put on Jesus in order to prevent living in the lusts of the flesh. We must prepare ahead of time. We must be willing to start early if we expect to make no provision or opportunity for the flesh later on. If we lack foresight, our lives will be filled with the enemy's plunder and we will lose much of our inheritance. It is for this point that I truly want to proclaim the truths in this book. It is time to think ahead rather than endeavor to plead with our teens about merely "waiting until marriage." The real question is: *what are we saving until marriage - merely the final act of sexual consummation?* When the Word of God is declared, there is hope, for our ignorance is revealed and the truth fills up the void of our minds.

In the writing of any book there are acknowledgments. Though I first taught on this topic in 1975, it was in October and November of 1977 that I first taught a series of Bible studies to youth regarding "dating and courtship". I owe much to the teens who came to these studies. It was a Saturday evening Bible Study for teenagers, and after I announced the topic more than 60 came the first night. The second night there were more than 100 in attendance, and we kept this attendance up for five consecutive Saturday evenings (over 120 one night), crowding into the living room of a family in Pembroke, Massachusetts. There was literally no room to move in their home! The hunger in these teens for the truth drew out of me the boldness to dare to declare it. I am forever grateful.

I also owe much to the teenagers and parents later in The New Testament Christian School who not only embraced the truths but were willing to embrace a vision for their children's children and go forth to minister as a team of adults and youth declaring a message of purity. My most memorable moments as an adult youth leader have come in vans, at restaurants, and in other such places where the Biblical alternative to dating has been practiced. The joy of discussing deep subjects with teenagers is a thrill I will always remember.

There are heartaches as well. Over the years it has been apparent that the immediate hunger for Biblical convictions among teens can be short lived when parents do not practice the truths at home, or young people merely want to pretend to be something they are not truly living in their hearts. Hypocrites are judged severely in the Bible. The consequences of professing a conviction in front of others and then falling away from its truth are devastating. God keeps His Word, and He holds us to our vows. It has been worse for those who once declared the truth and have turned aside than for those who never declared it at all. The stories of blessing and cursing only confirm the Bible however, and the conviction in my own heart of the truths of this book are stronger 25 years later than when they were first declared!

Many of the parents who have embraced this truth and been willing to face ridicule from others have been a blessing and reward beyond words. I salute every Dad that has been willing to "court his daughter" and every Mom who has given up that fantasy-land dream of seeing her son or daughter dating like she did. Without parental foundations laid and practiced in the home, the results among teens would be small and even more short-lived.

That is why it gives me great thrill and appreciation to have the Preface of this book written by Dick, Cheryl and Erin Doherty. Erin was 15 when she first voluntarily embraced the truths in this book. She had a vision then for her children's children, and retains that today. What a joy to see her develop, wrestle through the tests of a protected courtship, and join the faculty of our Christian school five years after she graduated! Her love of missions may take her far away from her family, but the truths of God's Word will always be close to her heart as she continues to surrender to her Lord. It is an honor to have her so openly write an updated preface *"ten years later"*.

Erin's, Dick and Cheryl, have embraced these truths for many years, and they have watched all four of their teens wrestle with the truths declared by them as they faced the vast sweeping current of "mainstream" Christianity after high school, where so few have even heard of Biblical purity. There are no perfect teenagers, and they would be the first to admit the faults of parenting that they and all of us have experienced. However, it is rare to have a family train their children in such a way that the oldest (such as Erin) can set such a precedent for the three younger ones. Yet this is what pioneering is all about. Their updated preface is also included, yielding the experience and wisdom that they have gained over the years.

I salute my precious wife, Charlene, for her undying support over the years when many of the truths declared by her husband were not readily received. I am forever grateful to my son, Jonathan, who has been willing to join with his Dad in ministry and be a friend and young man ready to lift up a standard. To my daughter, Shauna, who at a young age embraced a love for her Dad's "dates" and has stayed true to her own convictions; I will always be grateful.

Thank you, Rob Fantoni, for doing the tireless job of editing and proof-reading, and more importantly, for being willing to embrace the task of picing up the torch and sharing these truths to a new generation of youth.

May God give you a vision and hope of embracing the same truths so that you might lift up a standard against the flood tide of evil in our generation.

Paul W. Jehle
January, 2001

Preface of 1990 Edition - by Erin Doherty (age 15)
"A Word to Teenagers from a Teenager"

Dating. Sex. Petting. Kissing. Such words are magnetic, drawing one's eyes to read further on the subject. Those teenagers who are immune to desiring the happiness that a member of the opposite sex can bring are few. To be sure, there is nothing wrong with such emotions. The wrong is committed when we allow these emotions to get out of control and cause us to act with innate animalistic instincts, engaging in premarital sexual activity and stirring up passions that quickly become an engulfing flame.

We may have the best of intentions and resolve to wait until marriage, maintaining relatively high standards, but when the moment of temptation comes, will we be able to keep ourselves pure? I have asked myself this question many times. I have come to the conclusion that if I focus only on temporal things and short-term pleasures, I will fail when tested. I will fail unless I have a long-term goal, for *"where there is no revelation, the people cast off restraint."* (Proverbs 29:18).

We must start by gaining a vision for future generations. This means joining three or four generations together in unity. I know that the world says it's "uncool" to hang around your "old man" or be a "mama's boy", and that they feel the best place for your grandparents is in a nursing home, out of the way. But did God intend for us to become prone to the age barrier, keeping our distance from anyone several years older or younger than we? Did He mean for each generation to struggle through its own problems alone, with no help from those who are wise from experience? I do not believe so.

The Old Testament gives some excellent advice concerning this topic: *"Though one may be overpowered, two can defend themselves. A cord of three strands is not easily broken"* (Ecclesiastes 4:12). There have been times when I have learned lessons the hard way through going through them personally, for I frequently possess the "superiority" attitude that often is a characteristic of teenagers. I sometimes feel that I know more than my parents, who have simply forgotten what it's like to be a teen.

What a blessing it has been, though, when I have been willing enough to listen to my parents' or teachers' advice and have been spared much heartache and pain. In fact, it is through hearing testimonies from those older than I that inspired me to embrace God's standards. I had doubts that any system besides dating would be possible, but seeing the final products of happily married couples who waited for God's best has convinced me that it can work.

Not to say that it is easy. Believe me, with all of the sensuality that the world is flirting with, it is difficult not to be affected emotionally by all of the lustful images portrayed in commercials, movies, magazines, etc. It is even harder to abstain from such sin when the majority of your peers seem to be having the time of their lives: experiencing their first kiss, going to a prom with the cutest guy or most popular girl around, or going steady with someone special. What we must realize, though, is that the consequences of the dating pattern leave their mark on those who practice it.

Who knows about the rejection that follows a breakup except those that go through it? Who but the unwed mother who makes the decision knows the agony of being forced to give her baby up for adoption? Who understands the betrayal and worthlessness that one feels after having given up their virginity until it is too late?

We must learn to sacrifice temporal pleasures for eternal gain. The thrill of having obeyed God's commands far exceeds any thrill of sexual acts. I go to a small Christian school in which the ratio of girls to boys is about 2 to 1, and at times there has only been one boy in the high school. It's hard sometimes to sacrifice the interaction between boys and girls, when at another school there are many to choose from, but I feel that it's worth it.

I have found it helpful to look at sex and the other great benefits of marriage as a great big present wrapped with a "do not open until December 25" tag on it. We all remember what it was like as a young child to walk around the Christmas tree, trying to guess what was in each uniquely shaped box and wondering what kind of pleasure it will bring us. There are always those who just can't wait, and feel compelled to peel away just one tiny edge of the paper. Of course, the suspense mounts, and before long, the gift is completely revealed. The disappointment of knowing that there will not be any surprise on Christmas Day and the frustration brought about from the impatient act ruin the pleasure that the child would have received if he had waited.

Virginity is almost nonexistent in our generation. Those who aren't "experienced" are mocked and ridiculed by their friends, classmates, and peers. I am not willing to give in to such pressures, though, for I realize that at any given moment, if I so choose, I could become like the others, *but never again can they become like me.* I realize that God has His Sovereign Hand on some special man whom He is preparing to be my future husband, and if I want to cause our union to be the most sacred, fulfilling, and simply more than I have ever dreamed of, I must wait.

Of course, I could settle for second best and give in to a few kisses or sexual foreplay ahead of time, though not going all the way, but if I wait until the marriage bed for the entire process, I will be blessed beyond compare. For I will have no scars of rejection to overcome. I will be able to completely trust my husband, telling him my deepest hopes and innermost secrets, and know that he will not betray me. I will have not have memories of past boyfriends to use to throw up into my mate's face when I am displeased with him, thereby injuring him and causing tension. Instead, I can lovingly confront him and it can be more easily received.

How will I meet my future husband or wife, you are probably asking? I, too, sometimes wonder. If the dating pattern is not God's answer, then what is? As you read this book, you will see the alternative to dating: *team ministry.* The primary unit making up a team should be one's family. Strong relationships founded on anchors of trust and unconditional love are the key to the unity of this team. Relationships between parents and children are especially important. Teenage daughters need a male figure in their lives, and if their fathers do not give them the natural affection that they need, they will turn to other boys or men instead.

My father and I have an excellent relationship. We know each other very well since we both think alike, look alike, and talk alike. I look forward to special times when he takes me out to dinner alone, and we have a chance to talk about how we've been doing.

Outside of the family, the school or church can become a team. One purpose of a team is to work towards a common objective. Instead of focusing on self-centered "fun and games youth group meetings", why not begin to move out in ministry? Go to the streets and witness, or visit the elderly, or disciple new converts! As we begin to get our minds off constantly looking for someone to snare sensually and rest in the Lord's will, doing His work, He will begin to open our eyes to a certain person. We will observe how they minister, what their giftings are, and the character qualities they possess. We will know that this is His will because He will bring a relationship to form naturally.

This may sound like a fairy tale to some, but God will reward you if you are faithful to keep His commandments. Meanwhile, how can we prepare ourselves for our future mate? One woman who is now a happily married housewife was recently sharing her testimony and said that as a teenager she used to ask her family members what flaws in her character needed to be mended. We rarely take advantage of such experiences when we adopt the world's attitude toward our family. As her family members pinpointed her weaknesses, she was able to work at them in her daily life.

Lesson Six entitled "Cultivating True Friendships," is about forming deep relationships now with members of your own sex. I know that in the four years that my best friend and I have known each other, I have grown tremendously. Our weaknesses and strengths cause us to balance perfectly. Our relationship is a give and take one, in which we learn to contribute something to a relationship rather than just getting something out of it.

I pray that you, as a teenager, will read this book and begin to see the necessity of lifting up God's standards over the world's practices. As God reveals to you a long-term vision and grants you the strength to consider the eternal more valuable than the temporal, I hope that you, too, will see the need to embrace full purity.

As you move out in team ministry, may His Spirit reveal the one who fulfills your deepest dreams, and in future years may you join with him or her as an impenetrable team that cannot be broken apart.

Updated Preface to the 2001 Edition:
One Decade Later.... Still Seeking God's Perfect Will
by Erin Doherty, (age 25) - January, 2001

When recently asked to update the preface to *Dating vs. Courtship* which I wrote ten years ago as a 15-year-old girl, I first reread the earlier preface which I had written. The words struck home to me, reverberating in my inmost being as I realized again the truth behind the convictions which I had expressed during high school, centered primarily on the godly principles for relationships which Mr. Jehle elaborates upon in the following pages.

Over the past ten years my life experiences have broadened, often in ways I would never have predicted had you asked me several years ago. Since my teen years, I attended Hillsdale College in Michigan, graduating with a degree in Christian Studies and fully intending to dabble in journalism for a short time while waiting for God to join me to a mate. I had visions of the two of us then pouring our souls out in mission work or some other form of ministry, while raising a family of God-fearing children who would grow into men and women of conviction.

Life suddenly became slightly difficult and confusing when I formed a close friendship with a young man at college. It is easy to begin to wonder if a fulfilling friendship may turn into something more, when you feel ready for that stage in your life. I began ignoring warning signs that it would not end in marriage, and I turned a deaf ear at first to advice from family or friends who were concerned I was heading for heartache by not simply accepting this friendship for what it was.

But God had very different plans for me, and for him. Eventually we realized we were being led into different areas of service. I was interested in short/long-term missions work, potentially overseas, and in other types of full-time ministry, including teaching.

Later, when he met and married the woman God had planned for him, I was overwhelmingly grateful that I had not made a mistake in stepping outside of what I finally saw clearly that God had for me, and that he had been free to step into the relationship God had for him soon after we ended our friendship. It takes awhile sometimes to get over the human pity party of losing a good friend in a situation like that, but how freeing it is to know that instead of struggling with major regrets, both friends are able to simply enjoy the good memories they had shared, and move on as better people because of how they had grown.

I share this personal experience with you openly as a lesson and as a warning. Even following godly, wholesome principles for relationships, similar to those described in *Dating vs. Courtship*, does not guarantee any of us will never be disappointed, or even in some cases, devastated, if things do not go according to how we, in our limited, finite comprehension of God's best for us, first envision them.

Yet think of the heartache involved if we do not protect ourselves by embracing the convictions in this book you are about to read. Had I been involved physically rather than emotionally, or had we robbed each other through selfish demands rather than forming a strong friendship centered on God, who knows what heartaches or regrets either of us would feel now that God has led us in vastly different directions?

It is often difficult to know what God is saying or where He is ultimately leading us while viewing a relationship through the eyes of emotion, especially when it is based on a good, fulfilling friendship. Because of this, it is imperative that we go out of our way to insure that our regrets will be minimal and our learning experience positive if God suddenly shows us this relationship is to end as we know it. Under the protection of courtship principles, even through failure to at first see where God is directing, we will be protected from the greater consequences that might stall, hinder, or thwart the timing and purpose of God's plan for the rest of our lives.

Heartaches are at times a part of life because none of us is perfect and we aren't always as spiritually discerning as we should be. Sometimes it takes awhile to work out emotions and realize exactly where a relationship is headed, and risk is involved as your heart is put on the line during the process. *Yet if we build the fence far enough from the cliff, our failings do not have to take us over to consequences we must live with the rest of our lives.*

God is a jealous God, wanting the first fruits of our hearts and wanting the best for His beloved. He is concerned first of all that we are receptive to *His* wooing of our most passionate, intimate parts. Until we learn that lesson, we will grow discontent over time with any earthly relationship. Desiring any man or woman to meet and provide for what only God can give us will lead to heartache, disillusionment, and conflict.

The purpose of any human relationship should be to draw both people closer to God. When the relationship becomes inward and obsessive, it grows unhealthy and perverted very rapidly, for the attention is drawn to the created rather than the Creator. It becomes a simple matter of how each of you can get your needs met, rather than a question of how you can learn to better meet the needs of the other so that you can both move out in the gifts God has placed within you, covering each other's weaknesses and improving the other's strengths.

My students ask me if I want to get married or if I want to just spend my life on the mission field somewhere pouring my soul into natives or students. I have to laugh at the black-and-white nature of the question. I want to give what every woman wants to give - I want to find fulfillment in relationships, and find myself in a truly intimate and loving primary relationship with my soul mate someday. But I must be content resting in God's timing. It is best not to find oneself in a relationship and at that point be trying to figure out who you are or what you are supposed to do with your life. I want to grow to maturity in my identity as a single person, and then either be joyfully surprised with the unexpected gift of the treasured heart of a Godly man, or else spend my life bearing spiritual fruit that reflects my passionate walk with my Creator.

In recent months, when at times I desire a close friendship with someone of the opposite sex, or think perhaps I feel almost ready to marry, God has brought back into focus the supportive role my family still plays in my life, and brought my attention back to my Godly father who has been a consistent role model to protect, love, and teach me. He has filled my heart with contentment in knowing that my place right now is to be teaching in a Christian high school, nurturing the students as He trains me to be a mentor, friend, and mother.

These lessons of waiting on God's timing, protecting your heart through covenant relationships with your family, and keeping busy serving God in the meantime are part of what Mr. Jehle discusses in the upcoming chapters. I encourage you to internalize these principles, so that when your own life experiences unfold (often in ways you do not anticipate!), you are better prepared to navigate through the often deceptive maze of the human heart.

The wise author of Proverbs wrote the following verse: *"The mind of man plans his way, but the Lord directs his steps"* (Proverbs 16:9). God will be God despite our hearts' rebellious longings for ways other than His own. May God bless you as you read the following pages and learn the joy in allowing Him to direct your steps in your relationships!

A Word from Erin's Parents: Dick and Cheryl Doherty - **January, 2001**

We had the privilege of contributing a preface to the first edition of *Dating vs. Courtship* when our children ranged in age from 7 to 15 years. As parents, we had studied and even taught some of the material included in the book at workshops with our two older daughters in the late 1980's. We endeavored to lay a foundation in our family to encourage our children to pursue a course consistent with God's Word and will, a path contrary to prevailing trends and practices in relating to the opposite sex and seeking their mates.

The past ten years have been an experience in attempting to apply in practice what we believe God teaches in the area of relationships for youth and young adults. What we knew in principle was often put to the test in real situations as high school gave way to college or post college experiences and the teen years led to the early and mid 20's. Our roles as parents have shifted from directing to guiding, and now coaching and encouraging our children. One thing God has shown us over and over during this time is His faithfulness and the truth of His Word as it relates to courtship.

Dating vs. Courtship challenges both youth and parents to examine our beliefs and behavior in this critical area. Parents, don't just give this book to your young people and tell them to read it; take the time to read and meditate on the truths included here for yourself. Where it applies to you, acknowledge the errors in your own thinking and modeling before your children and commit before God to lead them toward Godly relationships.

Paul Jehle exposes myths and ungodly reasoning, outlines methods and practical guidelines, and prophetically proclaims a Biblical alternative to the world's standard of dating. We especially encourage parents to renew your thinking in this critical area. God desires to restore what the enemy has perverted and rebuild the foundation for future generations. You are a major link in God's plan to transmit these truths to your children and ultimately to future generations. The scriptural command of Romans 12:2; *"and be not conformed to this world; but be ye transformed by the renewing of your mind, that ye may prove what is that good, acceptable, and perfect will of God,"* is our exhortation to all who read this book. May God bless you as you endeavor to live these truths and walk in obedience to Him.

Lesson One

REBUILDING THE FOUNDATION
OF MANY GENERATIONS

As the young people piled into my living room week after week I pondered what it would take to have the kind of godly youth generation talked about in the Bible. I saw them sitting on the floor, poking, winking and distracting one another as I listened to myself play the accordion and lead the singing for the evening. Not many really sang, (at least that was the feeling I got). After the Bible study, I played policeman and broke up the couples in the cars, or back in the woods, who told their parents to come one hour later than the meeting actually ended so they could have some fun together.

It seemed like I was quite a legalist after all as the parents had accused me since I enforced my teachings against dating, dancing and rock music. However, I knew that God was after something much greater if only they (the youth) would keep themselves for His purposes.

It would seem that the teaching fell on deaf ears. The parents did not want to hear it, and the teens seemed powerless to fulfill the Word they heard. Breaking up couples on bike hikes, ski trips and all-night youth parties seemed routine and pretty soon I was known as the one who would actually publicly make a spectacle of those who "made out" during activities. I remember the nights I sat on my bed, or knelt, asking God what it would take to stem the tide. My tears became my bread and food as I cried out for a generation of purity. My answer came in an unusual way one day in mid-afternoon as I sat in my small office.

A tear ran down her cheek as she sat silently before me. Finally, she got up the courage to ask me the question that plagued her mind.

"Does God," she slowly began, "answer prayer when you are truly repentant?"

"It depends on what you mean," I replied, not willing to be put into any box in this situation. I could only guess why she had suddenly

1

asked to see me quite urgently in the middle of the afternoon. However, being the youth leader, it was not uncommon to have someone want to see you suddenly for one reason or another.

"What I want to know," she began again, "is whether God will perform a miracle in order to help me through a certain situation".

I was beginning to catch on. "What kind of a situation?", I answered rather calmly. Then it all came out.

"1 am pregnant a few weeks, and I want to know if God will take the baby home to be with Him rather than having me have to have it" she blurted out. "If God is a God of love, wouldn't He want to give me grace rather than punish me?" I was silent for a moment, both for her sake and mine.

"I made just one mistake," she said, "how could He let me get pregnant?"

As I pondered what my response would be, I realized that I would not be spending a great deal of time counseling her since our standards and policies avoided men counseling women, especially alone. I realized, however, that the situation I found myself in was critical for her. She trusted me, that was evident. What I was about to say might alter her desire for more counseling and follow up. God loved her. He loved her no less than when she was a virgin. However, her cry for help only magnified the thinking of the day. She desperately wanted to apply a false and deceptive idea of Biblical grace - the taking away of the consequences of sin.

I thought of the teachings I had given only two years before. She had thought I was quite "square" and her parents had agreed. When I had completed a set of teachings on why dating was not the kind of practice in which Christians should be involved she was almost indignant.

"Is God against my having fun?" she had asked. "Are Christians supposed to marry ugly men and go to mission fields?"

Her parents were even more upset. They thought I was very legalistic to think that teenagers should refrain from kissing, embracing and "making out." After all, it had worked out fine for them, so they encouraged her in the typical dating pattern, but to simply be careful and cautious.

"God does not erase the consequences of our actions," I began slowly. "In fact, He allows them to teach us things nothing else could accomplish as successfully. One of the most powerful lessons, and one of the most painful, you are experiencing now." I could tell that as I spoke it was really sinking in. "Though He loves you just the same, and has completely forgiven you if you have truly repented, you have reaped what you have sown both in your lifestyle and habits of yielding to passion and temptation. You are simply now fulfilling the consequences of your thinking. You did not make just one mistake. The mistake occurred months before you ever went too far on a date. It occurred the moment you thought there was no need to guard yourself from the first sinful thought. God will give you the grace and mercy to overcome; and whether you give the child up for adoption or intend to raise it by yourself or with your family, God will also give the grace necessary to help your child understand as he or she grows up why there may not be a Daddy around."

During my answer she only looked at the carpet. Tears flooded her eyes. I felt some of my own. "Oh, God," I thought, "how many teens must go through such tragedy?" Her future was now totally altered. She was not just looking forward to graduation, but a baby! A baby! Should she put the child up for adoption, or should she become another single parent? I prayed that abortion would not be an option in her mind. The cold consequences seemed to override the obvious need for God's grace. Though God would work all things out for good, her life would never be the same and she knew it. I determined then and there to never alter, compromise or set aside the highest call and vision God has for teens. I had my answer from the Lord. Unless I was willing to preach a higher vision, deeper calling and greater destiny, there would be no reason why teenagers would restrain themselves from selling their eternal calling for temporary moments of pleasure.

That counseling situation, (though not exactly the way it happened to protect the individual involved) could be repeated a hundred fold around the country with youth leaders and pastors. It is not unique, nor is it totally out of the ordinary. I began teaching on the dangers of the dating pattern in 1975. 1 felt that something had to be done to prevent sin rather than simply asking God to help us correct it all the time, but parents seemed more unwilling to heed the warning than did the teenagers. The rushed weddings, the broken hearts and crippled futures our teenagers were facing only added to my burden. Later in life to see some of the same ones get divorces, be beaten by their husbands, or left scarred and almost ruined by age 24, was devastating to me. Something had to be done.

Truth had to be declared!

Our Current State of Affairs

As I review this book, it is the year 2000. A decade of destiny still awaits the teenagers born since 1982 who have graduated this year. Our present teenage generation, born since 1973, has had to live as millions of their contemporaries were killed before they were born. Abortion, infanticide and other evils are snuffing out their peers before they ever breathe the air on this planet. Those who live face drugs, violence and immorality with the price tag of AIDS.

Someone is after them. Someone wants to destroy them. This is no joke. We know that Satan has always wanted youth. He knows that they are the greatest enemy he faces if they would wake up.

God says that youth are *"ordained strong because of their enemies"* (Psalm 8:2) and are arrows in the hands of adults, being God's reward (Psalm 127:3-5). It is the young men who are known for overcoming the wicked one (1 John 2:13-14). Thus, Satan's all-out attack is on the youth. This increases as we near God's hour when the greatest revival of youth will occur alongside one of the greatest flood-tides of evil the world has ever seen.

Satan knows the strength of the family. It is the strongest area of the Kingdom of God. It is the place where the future generations are prepared to inherit God's glory and continue His Church on the earth. Satan must have the next generation in order to continue his havoc on earth. He can stand to lose one generation, but not several! That is why God in the last days will *"turn the heart of the fathers to the children, and the heart of the children to the fathers"* (Malachi 4:6).

If Satan can destroy the preparation for marriage among the teens and anyone who is single, he can then destroy the marriage and home

4

much easier since the gaping holes in the foundation are easy entrances for his devices, and through deception they meet with little resistance.

What kind of generation do we face? Is it that serious? The national statistics are telling the story, but some are so blind they cannot see the seriousness of the situation. During the twenty-five years I have been teaching teenagers on dating vs. courtship the situation has grown steadily worse. What was once considered yielding to temptation is now viewed as normal practice on dates. It is no longer whether one restrains his passions, but whether one can avoid getting a disease due to his normal sexual activity. Prevention is considered to be figuring out how not to reap the consequences of one's actions rather than changing one's lifestyle.

Since the 1970's national statistics have shown that premarital sex has skyrocketed in astronomical terms. Virginity is out; sexual activity is in. As an example, consider this report from a local newspaper that also reflects the state of the nation statistically:

> *"Two high schoolers are on a date, and the boy wants more than a few kisses. The girl resists, saying she isn't ready for sex. The boy pleads, tries to talk her into it, as he has for several dates. She finally gives in, thinking maybe she owes him that much and maybe she'll otherwise lose his love.*
>
> *"It is a common scenario today, as it has been for years, according to Cape teenagers and adult counselors. But some of the teens, while not necessarily condoning the coercion, see it as a normal state of affairs.*
>
> *"After all, they say, the couple under discussion has been 'going out,' or seeing each other exclusively, for three months. Three months? Is that a long time to go out before expecting intercourse? 'Oh, yeeeaaaahhh,' a group of Cape high school students chorus.*
>
> *"..nationwide the incidence of 'date rape' has escalated, as youths continue to question exactly what*

rape is, whether saying 'no' really means 'no' and whether it is right to resist.

"National and state statistics on teen sexuality, quoted by several local and national sources, are telling:

- Ninety percent of males, 80 percent of females are sexually active by age 18.

- More than 1 million teenagers get pregnant each year. About 40 percent of those pregnancies end in abortion; 13.3 percent in miscarriages.

- Twenty or 30 years ago, a large majority of pregnant teenagers put their babies up for adoption; today, a large majority keep the babies even though many teen-age mothers must drop out of school.

- One in five girls nationwide will be raped on a date, but only about 5 percent of such incidents are reported. The most frequent victims of date rape are aged 17 to 19.

- Fifty percent of all teenagers believe it is OK to force sex.

"'It's not fashionable to be a virgin. If you are, you don't admit it,' said Mary Lou Holland, a social worker for the Early Childbearing program in Falmouth, who counseled about 75 pregnant teenagers from the Upper Cape last spring.

"'It's almost an expectation now. Twelve-year old boys are kidded if they haven't had sex,' added program director Michelle Bums. 'We can deny it and deny it, but kids are sexually active, and we have to deal with it"[1]

How do we prepare for solid marriages when 80 to 90 percent of the youth population will not be virgins when they marry? Eighty to

---

[1] Driscoll, Kathi, *Cape Cod Times*, Monday, September 5, 1988; page 5, the fourth part in a series on pressures faced by today's teens.

ninety percent! I hope that has sunk in. We're not talking about a few people giving in to sin, we are talking about an epidemic of sin that is ruining the future marriages of our nation and the world. It is well known that, as a result of our sexual activity, puberty is beginning at earlier and earlier ages. I believe it is a result of God's judgment built into the physical body for our reckless ignorance of His standards. If sex is cheap, so is one's body and soul. The animal instincts simply take over (like date rape) and one is reduced to an existence of survival hardly ready for the challenges that await the world in the future.

Thorns and Broken Walls

America was not always this sinful. Oh, there has always been sin; but not so openly demonstrated and arrogantly paraded as normal living. What was once shameful and to be hid from public view has now become a proud display of rebellion toward God's standards. How did we get this way? What are the causes and consequently the solutions? Is there a way we can understand what has happened, especially in the church? I believe God has a clear picture for us to consider when viewing today's generation.

> *"I went by the field of the slothful, and by the vineyard of the man void of understanding; and lo, it was all grown over with thorns, and nettles had covered the face thereof, and the stone wall thereof was broken down. Then I saw, and considered it well: I looked upon it, and received instruction. Yet a little sleep, a little slumber, a little folding of the hands to sleep: so shall thy poverty come as one that travelleth, and thy want as an armed man."* - Proverbs 24: 30-34

Thorns Instead of Fruit

The field God ordained to bring forth fruitfulness in our lives is filled with thorns due to our slothfulness. Sloth is word that basically means laziness and apathy. Our lack of diligence is what leaves a

7

vacuum and void for weeds and thorns to grow. Thorns are the worldly influences that choke off fruit (Matthew 13:7,22).

Certainly we could focus in on the fact that the state of the average marriage, even Christian marriage, is like a field grown over with thorns and with little protection from its enemies of lust, fornication, divorce and adultery. Why? It is because, due to our slothfulness, we have allowed thorns to grow instead of fruit.

Thorns grow because no one removes weeds. Thorns are also planted by us in our negligence.

Oh, that we could wake up!

A Breach in the Wall

When God created the human race He built moral walls and boundaries into His creation. If God is the only one who is God, then man must be limited, finite and in need of boundaries. The boundaries are for his good, his success and happiness.

No matter how many individuals take an opinion poll about how they like the boundaries or walls and whether they wish to obey them, all will pay the penalty for ignoring them. When we ignore these moral walls built into our bodies and our lifestyles, the slothfulness described above takes its toll and brings with it God's judgment in the way of the consequences we reap. Our slothfulness is exhibited today by the many holes in our walls (or lack of standards) in relation to our preparation for marriage.

Today we rarely think ahead. We simply live by the moment, desiring to know what to say to our children after they are tempted or have fallen. What about preparing ahead? Why not build the walls that will protect them as the foundation is being laid in their lives?

Sleeping Instead of Preparing

The years just prior to marriage for most individuals are the teen years. These are the years of preparation. In other generations when marriages took place close to the onset of puberty the years preceding those were preparation years. No matter how one looks at it, preparation is critical for marriage to be successful.

In the picture above, instead of preparing we have a habit of sleeping. It is in this preparation area, prior to marriage, where we are sleeping the most. It is also one of the primary reasons this book is being written. Oh, that God would help us prepare instead of sleeping that we might experience greater success!

Poverty and Need

The verses of Scripture above picture for us yet another evidence of the decay of slothfulness. This evidence is poverty and great need. Today we are very poor in relation to purity and virginity. Virginity is more than "waiting until marriage". It is the inheritance a woman and man bring to their marriage bed of passionate love. Today we are stripped of this, having given it away to many when it was reserved for only one. As indicated above, our poverty is like a restless traveler who never has a home. Passionate love was never meant to travel from one person to another; it was meant to rest at home, with only one individual. Our need is now like an armed man. The needs for purity have become fortresses with locked doors. In other words, our weakness to fornication has become an armed man in our midst! In order to restore purity and virginity, we must now fight! Yet, our fighting must include preparation and forethought in order to win a decisive victory!

How long will we simply set ourselves back a generation before waking up out of our sleep? Why do we always have to rebuild the walls instead of building them the right way in the beginning? Why do we have to continue to ask for understanding as to why we are being defeated rather than winning the battles in the name of the Lord? What will it take to prepare properly? Is there a generation of parents who will be willing to repent of the way they did not prepare and apologize to their teens for setting them back a generation in God's purposes? Is there a generation of teenagers on the earth who will pay the price while they are young in order to go further than any other adult generation in the history of the world has gone in seeing God's purposes fulfilled?

In this book, God's vision and standard will be revealed, but only you who are reading can answer the above questions in your own heart.

Some Root Causes for our Present Dilemma

At a quick glance, we can see that the situation is serious. Yet, how many look beyond the sexual activity to its cause and roots? Why are young people feeling so cheap about themselves? Why do they want love so desperately that they will trade it for animalistic lust and forced rape just to get somewhat close to love's ellusive feeling?

A Self-Centered Gospel

Whether we like it or not, in our generation we have been captured by psychological humanism. It has tainted the way we have viewed everything. Since we have not been trained in discerning its roots and patterns of thinking, we have been easily deceived about God, man and marriage, embracing humanistic premises.

Some characteristics of what is meant by a self-centered Gospel are:

1. <u>Man-centered Christianity</u> where half-truths are overemphasized such as Jesus is *my* Savior. He died for *me*. He will meet *my need*. But Christianity doesn't begin with me, it begins with Christ.

While these are certainly true in context and balance, we have forgotten that He chose us before we chose Him. We have lost the emphasis on Lordship and obedience. Thus, we have felt that life is primarily for our pleasure, enjoyment and fun when this is not the case. Life is primarily for God's glory and purposes; not yours or mine. I am saved to fulfill His purposes, not for Him to bless my purposes. Thus, marriage is not for my own purposes and happiness primarily, but it is for His purposes.

2. <u>External pleasure over internal preparation</u> has also been improperly emphasized. Thus, why not have fun dating and habitually yielding to temporal pleasure?

The time for internal character building and seriousness is later, we rationalize. However, true Christianity emphasizes that the internal heart condition is the cause of external actions and conditions. The way I prepare or do not prepare now will have a part to play in the type of life I am able to live later on. In other words, we reap what we sow.

3. <u>"I need no laws since I am saved by grace"</u> is one of the most devastating deceptions of our age.

Grace never did away with the Law! Grace is God's ability given to us so that we can keep the law! We are not saved from law, we are saved from sin!

The purpose of God's Law is to keep us from destruction and help us reap the greatest blessings in life. This misunderstanding of grace and law has given license to much sinful activity (often in the name of Christianity) and helped to water down standards for the past several generations. We have more than paid for the consequences.

4. <u>A lack of responsibility and accountability</u> has been the result of these humanistic thought-patterns.

We have not realized that our actions today will affect generations after us. We never think of generations after us since we are so consumed with the here and now. We have the problems we have today because previous generations did not restrain themselves. The importance of the inheritance we have received, and the one we will give, is lost on a generation consumed with receiving and selfishness.

We are accountable to God and can cause many future generations either great blessings, or heartache and bondage, due to our obedience or disobedience to God and His Word. Humanistic teaching always de-emphasizes our responsibility and accountability to God.

The Destruction of the Family

It is a fact that young people who often cry out for the attention of a boyfriend or girlfriend do so out of a void in their own family - a missing influence, especially the father. Others do not have a complete family, and some could not define one if they were to try since they have never experienced the security of such a unit. Still others have lost their family, having gone through divorce, separation or some other crisis. Though certainly many of these setbacks are not the deliberate fault of those involved, and can be overcome through God's grace and the church, there is still a greater potential for the following consequences when the family is out of God's order:

- *A lack of security* can form when there is no family heritage to serve as a foundation. These are the family traditions, habits and special events that constantly remind us that we are valuable and do have a place in life.

- *A lack of true love* exists when individuals have no natural affection from parents and other family members. With no reference or backdrop from which to define real love, individuals are left with the street reference dictionary which is written by those who are out to avenge their own lack of true love.

- *A lack of parental leadership* due to the improper or absent roles of father and mother. Teen-age daughters need their fathers desperately as do teen-age sons. If the father does not respect his daughter and take time to treat her with grace, she will try to find it somewhere else, only to be disappointed. If the father does not direct and lead his son in true manliness, he will find the bold leadership he is seeking in street gangs that demand high standards of loyalty and adventure, but in the context of sin and rebellion. It is also true with the mother's role as well. She often finds herself either trying to be Dad and Mom at once, or somehow trying to balance out the indifference of the father. Direction is hard to replace, (though it is possible in a tight church taking its responsibility of oversight in relation to broken homes), when a Dad is not fulfilling his role (see Exodus 20:12; Ephesians 6:1-4).

- *A lack of family vision* exists when life centers around individual activities, making money and other temporal pursuits. A family heritage and vision as to its purpose in the earth and the Kingdom of God, is full of adventure and will supply much of what is needed in the life of a young person. It was the family that was first given the "dominion mandate" to fulfill God's purposes in the earth (Genesis 1:26-28). Oh, that families would seek The Lord and discover their calling and role in manifesting the Kingdom of God once again! Their spiritual and genealogical history would give such heritage and meaning to youth!

The Lukewarm Church

The Church must accept its part of the blame as well. Young people are leaving churches by the droves, and the churches are trying to draw them in by giving them religious coatings over the same things they are involved in on the street. The young people are too smart for this. Why get a watered down version of sin in the church when I can get the real thing on the street? Our gimmicks are backfiring. We need to face it. Our feeble attempts to lure our teenagers through lukewarm, compromised standards are not working. They don't have a shred of evidence Biblically, either! Consider the results of the lukewarm church that dominates our culture today:

- *An acceptance of defeat* in relation to the teen years is probably one of the greatest sins the church faces in relation to youth. Instead of telling them the teen years are the years of harvest when they have the greatest opportunity with the least responsibility to damage the devil's kingdom and prepare for fulfilling God's plan, we repeat the devil's lie with a religious coat: "teen years are years of rebellion and self-identity crisis, but God is able to get you through them if you hang on to Him". If that is all the vision we can muster, why should we be shocked when they fulfill the lukewarm expectations we set before them?
- *The youth group* ranks up there with the mistakes we have made within the church. Here we group teens with their peers with a leader who must be able to relate to them, replace the father and mother's job

of building family heritage activities, and provide activities that often sneak Jesus in when they aren't looking. Often youth groups become pseudo-gangs where we replicate what is happening in the world, and neglect the very foundation needed for success - the parents! Thus, sin, destruction and rebellion lead the church replacing our Commander and Chief: the Lord Jesus. There is a better way. Our youth often know they are being ripped off, catered to as second class Christians. Why don't we take them where the action is in Christianity? Why always separate them from things that are serious, expecting them not to be interested? Instead, why not minister as families and churches, drawing those from broken homes into a context where they can be healed with the real thing rather than a counterfeit? Let us join the generations rather than always separating them with artificial boundaries given to us by tradition and secular psychology?

- *We have given our youth no adult heroes.* They have heard of Moses, Noah and Abraham and of course Jesus. Although these are Scriptural heroes, and necessary to portray, they are only vague theories unless someone in their life personifies the character, courage and faith of the Bible. Why not have adult heroes in the church take teens with them in all aspects of the Christian life so they are a team building the Kingdom together? This would help to offset the TV heroes and rock stars who fill the void for heroes in our day. It is about time we determined to return Dad and Mom to the status of hero for the next generation!

- *We have had no vision* or challenge within the church for our teenagers. What opportunities await them other than baby-sitting, spending time in the nursery or once a year participating in a youth service? Although these behind-the-scenes ministries are necessary to build an attitude of service, we must offer more than this in order for them to run with us and receive the baton of God's vision for reforming their lives and their generation. We need to begin to join the generations in everyday ministry rather than separating them all the time. We need to tell it like it is, right between the eyes, rather than trying to fool them. When a teenager enters an early eternity from drunk driving or lives with consequences of sexual diseases and

14

unfulfilled marriages, what can we say then about our inability and lack of courage and love to tell them the truth?

Thus, we need to begin to strengthen and clarify our view of the gospel, Christianity, the home and the church if we wish to see the teen years reap a harvest. Dating is not a side issue. It is the foundation for the future of the home and church in relation to embracing a Kingdom vision. We need to challenge Christian homes and churches to rebuild the vision God gave us in His Word. It is time to raise a standard higher rather than always lowering it to mediocrity. Let us set the vision high so that we might hit a higher mark and impact in earth for the advance of the Kingdom!

A Vision to Rebuild

God is calling young people today to prepare for His purposes in the earth. He is calling all of us to embrace a vision beyond our life time and even beyond the life time of our children's children so that we are committed to His purposes. We need to rebuild God's original purpose and vision. What are these purposes?

> *"And they that shall be of thee shall build the old waste places; thou shalt raise up the foundations of many generations; and thou shalt be called, the repairer of the breach, the restorer of paths to dwell in."* - Isaiah 58:12

Building the Old Waste Places

We need to rebuild the old waste places, or that which has been ruined by sin. We need to restore virginity and its glory. We need to restore purity, or "internal" virginity as well. This means we need to rebuild the character necessary to establish solid homes in the future so that we can defeat the enemy's plan to ruin humanity. Jesus will build His church, you can count on it, but wouldn't it be great to have several generations at one time being a part of it and consciously doing it His way?

Raising Up the Foundations of Many Generations

In order to raise up the foundation of many generations we need to first restore that foundation. The foundation of a generation is marriage. It is the foundation stone for bringing forth children who will understand their purpose in life. Though not everyone will marry, the principles necessary for forming solid relationships are related to the preparation process for marriage.

When the preparation for marriage is ruined (Biblical courtship) the marriage begins on the wrong foundation. It is building on sand rather than on a solid rock for many generations to come. The foundation we lay now will affect several generations in the future. It is time for both parents at home and leaders in the church take a good look at the future and prepare to build a solid foundation for our grandchildren to inherit.

Repairing the Breach

We need to repair the holes (or breaches) in the walls. These holes have let the enemy in time and time again. These holes, for our purposes in this book, are the patterns of dating we have accepted as standard tradition for years. They produce holes large enough for the enemy to build castles of destruction in our emotions. It is time a generation arose that was willing to rebuild the walls - those standards which are needed in order to keep the enemy out and build a new generation!

Finally, we need to remove the thorns and weeds in our pathway so that we can see clearly the direction in which to move. These paths represent for us the attitudes that we must embrace regarding our view of the opposite sex as well as our teenage years.

It is our testimony. Our testimony is ordained to be a fruitful demonstration that overcomes the enemy (see Revelation 12:11). Without a pure set of attitudes, it will be impossible to maintain any standards. If your desire is constantly to climb the wall, you will find a way. What we need is a restoration of the right attitudes (primarily surrendering to God's power within) toward life that will keep the weeds and thorns out of our way. We need to restore the testimony of God's keeping power in addition to His ability to save us from sinful bondages of the past. Let's restore these kinds of paths for future generations to walk in!

As you gain a vision for rebuilding the generations it will help you to govern your life and stay within God's prescribed guidelines for success. Only then will you be truly happy. Only then will the city of God have walls in the earth that keep the enemy out because of the great self-control exercised within. May God bless you as you accept the challenge to restore and rebuild the foundations of many generations.

> *"Where there is no vision, the people are unrestrained, but he that keepeth the law, happy is he."* - Proverbs 29:18

Lesson Two

THE FAILURE OF
THE DATING PATTERN

The words "date" and "dating" traditionally meant a "time and place" at which two individuals would get together. It has since been romanticized in novels, movies and television shows as two members of the opposite sex meeting in order to spend some aspect of passion. Initially, it was always assumed that one's date was in public and emphasized social endeavors and interests. Only when serious intentions were involved did the stage progress to "courtship" and even then couples did not go places alone.

Today the couple is alone immediately on a "date" with the goal to arouse passions. Though some would deny any such motives it is only a matter of honesty where one might disagree as to time and degree of arousing passions. In the church, we have simply put a moral limit upon the *amount of passion* as well as the *process of spending it* so that we would stop at some point short of its natural conclusion.

Below is a description of the synopsis of the modern dating pattern that usually occurs. It is not meant to be an actual diary of events, since times change and the application would have different meanings anywhere in the world. However, the pattern usually remains the same and is worthy of analysis.

Step One: Commonly Held Myths are Believed

Through the media of television, movies, books, magazines and the spoken and unspoken expectations of the adult generation the myths stated below and hosts of others are believed as the standard pattern of living. In Proverbs 6 and 7, God takes quite a bit of time to uncover the ignorance regarding the consequences of unholy relationships. All who stumbled for immediate sexual pleasure were "void of understanding".

"For at the window of my house I looked through my casement, and beheld among the simple ones, I discerned among the youths, a young man void of understanding" - Proverbs 7:6-7

In our society today, especially in America, there are myths which adults and consequently teens embrace that lead us into traps and keep us void of understanding. These attitudes must be exposed so that we can begin to unmask and discern the faulty foundation of the dating pattern.

Myth #1 - One of the greatest needs in my life is a boyfriend or girlfriend because it helps me overcome my loneliness and fulfill my social needs.

"If we say that we have fellowship with him, and walk in darkness, we lie, and do not the truth. But if we walk in the light, as He is in the light, we have fellowship with one another, and the blood of Jesus Christ his Son cleanseth us from all sin." - 1 John 1:6-7

God has designed fellowship with Him (as well as the Body of Christ) to fulfill our social needs and our temptations of loneliness. Loneliness becomes a sin when it becomes the reason why we do things. It is not overcome through dating anyway. Only repentance from the sin of self-pity and obedience to God overcomes the kind of loneliness that enslaves us. The real social need of individuals is to learn to fellowship and build relationships that are not sexual or sensual in nature. Having a boyfriend or girlfriend builds pressure in exclusiveness that is not only not needed - it hinders the fulfillment of the truly lonely person who needs a deeper relationship with Jesus and others in the church.

Myth #2 - A necessary part of growing up is having someone with whom you can share your affections and trust. Dating provides this type of fulfillment.

"Let love be without hypocrisy. Abhor what is evil; cling to what is good. Be devoted to one another in brotherly love; give preference to one another in honor" - Romans 12:9-10

The dating context is the worst atmosphere to honestly share your affections since it is love in hypocrisy, or sensual love disguised as true love. A good friend is not one that traps your emotions or leads you into an atmosphere where blindness can occur due to infatuation. A true friend is one that honors you. What we need is brotherly and sisterly affection and love from true friends that are not out to abuse our trust for the fulfillment of sexual desire. The kind of affection we need is brotherly and sisterly affection, not boyfriend and girlfriend affection that needs a date to be shared.

Myth #3 - Kissing, embracing and 'puppy love' is what the teen years are all about. However, pregnancy should be avoided, and one needs to draw the line and wait until marriage.

"But in a great house there are not only vessels of gold and of silver, but also of wood and of earth; and some to honor, and some to dishonor. If a man therefore purge himself from these, he shall be a vessel unto honor, sanctified, and meet for the master's use, and prepared unto every good work. Flee also youthful lusts; but follow righteousness, faith, charity, peace, with them that call on the Lord out of a pure heart." - II Timothy 2:20-22

"To every thing there is a season, and a time to every purpose under the heaven: ...a time to embrace, and a time to refrain from embracing.. - Ecclesiastes 3:1,5

The real question is: how much are you keeping until marriage? The above myth suggests you are saving the baby until marriage. Often this is shrouded in ignorance since it cannot be assumed that most teens understand basic biology and what causes pregnancy anyway. Also, this myth suggests that one simply needs to save sexual intercourse for marriage - but not all of the steps leading up to it. This is nonsense. If you are going to light the fires of passion, why should you save only the final step until marriage?

However, if you wish to be a truly honorable vessel unto the Lord, you prepare for that by purging yourself of all youthful lusts so that you have a pure heart for Him. One needs to save the emotions, affections and complete process until marriage or it will build habits and patterns of lust, sensuality and fornication that will be hard to break.

Myth #4 - It is cute to see 7 to 11 year olds pairing up and having crushes on classmates. It prepares them for the teen years when they will be going steady with someone and ultimately when they will find the one God has prepared for them. After all, that is the way we have done it as adults, and it hasn't hurt us! From a Christian point of view we do not take crushes seriously, it is only a cute thing to do.

> *"Be ye therefore followers of God, as dear children; and walk in love, as Christ also hath loved us, and hath given himself for us an offering and a sacrifice to God for a sweet-smelling savor. But fornication, and all uncleanness, or covetousness, let it not be once named among you, as becometh saints; neither filthiness, nor foolish talking, nor jesting, which are not convenient; but rather giving of thanks"* - Ephesians 5:1-4

To jest about the pairing up of our youth is like ignoring God's command to take forethought in guarding ourselves against fulfilling the lusts of the flesh (Romans 13:14). God commands that we abstain from all uncleanness and any jesting or talking that is not appropriate. We should rather be giving thanks that Jesus died to save us from these sins and help us prepare for His plan of establishing future generations through marriage that will fulfill the Great Commission in the earth.

Most adults who do not feel they have been harmed from the dating pattern are not comparing their present marriage or family to God's standard. You reap what you sow. To joke about what a nice couple two young people make and our constant expectation of all young people to be thinking sensually of the opposite sex is a testimony of how small our vision really is.

We may think it a joke, but the laws God built into the human body work anyway, and the devil will use every opportunity to derail God's purposes and have another teen generation waste its years of inheritance. One of the greatest distractions during the teen years is a sensual eye for the opposite sex - it keeps teens from a radical surrender to Christ and a focus on preparing for His call.

To practice this myth is to treat marriage and one's future mate like the purchase of a car. You test drive it to make sure you are compatible. Test driving the spending of passion doesn't work like a machine. People are living beings, and since sexual fulfillment is the final consummation, the real test is whether an individual can be friendly without flirting and spending passion - that is real preparation!

Myth #5 - One of the purposes of the church is to help our youth and single adults find their mates within the Christian community. That is why we encourage them having boyfriends and girlfriends within their church youth groups rather than from the world.

> *"And it came to pass, that after three days they found him in the temple, sitting in the midst of the doctors, both hearing them, and asking them questions. And all that heard him were astonished at his understanding and answers. And when they saw him, they were amazed; and his mother said unto him, 'Son, why hast thou thus dealt with us? behold, thy father and I have sought thee sorrowing. 'And he said unto them, 'How is it that ye sought me? wist ye not that I must be about my Father's business?"'* - Luke 2:46-49

The preparation of young people for marriage is one of God's purposes for the church. However, His method is not to set up the dating pattern within the church so that the same sinful patterns can be practiced upon believers instead of unbelievers. His pattern is to build within each young person the desire to ask meaningful questions about the purpose of life and their own destiny.

The primary concern of the teen years is to lay a foundation and practice of being about the Father's business. It is through this focus that we will be led by God to the individual God has for us who has the same desire and calling.

Myth #6 - Dating is so necessary because my parents do not understand me. They are old-fashioned. They think everything is supposed to be the way it was when they were young. Times have changed. I can't relate to anyone except someone of the opposite sex who really understands me and loves me.

> *"And they understood not the saying which he spake unto them. And he went down with them, and came to Nazareth, and was subject unto them; but his mother kept all these sayings in her heart. And Jesus increased in wisdom and stature, and in favor with God and man."* - Luke 2:50-52

Of any teenager who has ever lived, Jesus would have the greatest reason to testify that his parents did not understand him. In fact, the Scriptures state it just that simply. However, he still went home with his parents, was submissive to them, and waited until He was ready to minister and reach out to others. The reason parents sometimes do not understand teenagers is because they have no relationship with them. You never understand people you don't know.

The real solution is for youth to build relationships with their parents and other adults that will help them in difficult times. This is real maturity. One can't be always asking the same people who have the same questions as they do to give answers. Real maturity in the teen years is the kind of relationship with a mother and father that allows one to talk about anything, including sex, openly and in the right context and attitude.

Thus, the very foundation for the dating pattern consists of myths. We have built the entire edifice on a pile of sand. The myths we have listed could be expanded and I am sure each of us could add a hundred variations.

However, in summary, the dating process rests on myths that substitute sensual feeling for true fellowship; sensual affection for natural affection; premature passion for honor and respect; foolish jesting for gratefulness; our pleasure for His business; and peer relationships through pairing up for healthy relationships with parents, adults and peers together.

These commonly held myths only help to cover over the real problem. They take as their premise that all youth should give in to the temptations and natural feelings of their own bodies and souls. Somehow we embrace the idea that there are no teenagers or single adults alive who would ever buck the tide. We ignore the spiritual potential of the teen years and the real destiny God has for teenagers and single adults before they are married. There needs to be a challenge to rise above the norm and become all that God has for you now in preparation for marriage later on.

Probably the most erroneous premise in the above myths is the idea that whatever you do now will not be paid for later. Even the most happy marriages today can trace the scars they face to the dating pattern of their youth. Couples with unsatisfied sexual lives in marriage; husbands always looking at pretty ladies in the mall and flirting with secretaries; and wives who are always dreaming of what life would be like if they had a different husband - these are some of the results and scars of the patterns set earlier, during the preparation period. We need to expose the faulty foundation of dating and continue to understand the process so commonly followed today.

Step Two: Sensual Love is Encouraged

How is sensual love - or lust - encouraged? In a preteen, it may not begin by talking about sleeping with a boyfriend, but it begins by condoning "crushes" and the fact that one has a secret boyfriend. This is simply practicing a life of fantasy and in marriage later on it will continue as a secret fantasy lover. Adults and others encourage this by establishing fantasies as the standard rather than something that ought to be restrained.

For instance, it is not uncommon to have an adult add to what a young person states, leading one to continually think of sensual love rather than brotherly affection. When a young person states she has a friend and we ask - what *kind* of friend? Is he cute? This may seem to be innocent, but it plants seeds that the friends we expect them to choose also double for lovers. These seeds will eventually sprout. We should not be shocked when the plant is nourished and gives the potential fruit of a pregnant teenage girl at 14 years of age.

Parents should be careful when there is any unusual fascination or imagination toward members of the opposite sex or their own sexual body parts. One way to avoid this is to simply speak of body parts by their appropriate names when children are young. In this way they do not think that their "private parts" are evil or ugly, but simply private and not to be discussed openly or in public. Any aspect of sensual (rather than natural) attraction for sexual body parts (their own or others) should give us warnings and cause us to correct the situation.

Step Three: Pairing Up

As preteens grow up, it is a common practice to look for someone with which to pair up. Usually it begins with notes, cards and secrets that someone is "more than a friend" - a boyfriend or girlfriend. This pairing up is accompanied by flirting (from eyebrows, an inordinate desire for make-up and vanity magazines, to having someone notice the way you walk, talk, or dress), shallow talk that has as its real motive and goal the getting of another individual's attention.

It is important to recognize that pairing up is not simply two people talking or fellowshipping with one another. It is the *motive* that creates an *atmosphere* of sensual passion, and it is usually detected by others and invisible to the ones practicing it. There is a clear difference in posture, eye contact, tone of voice and attitude that distinguishes two individuals talking and a pair that are spending passion.

The teenager doesn't need notes or any other type of subtle activity. They simply pair up, first internally, and then externally. One usually sees two individuals spending more time together - at first within the group of friends that he or she has had for some time. Whether it is called "going steady" or "simply friends," usually it is obvious to the other friends that a couple has been identified.

Step Four: Isolation

As a couple begins to "date," which does not at all mean that they have to go somewhere together, they spend more and more time thinking, dreaming and simply being together in their emotions. Dates occur all the time in the imagination, but the goal is to spend more and more time together physically in order to act out what has been fantasized through emotional involvement.

At this step a certain isolation begins to occur, which is often accepted by peers because of the normal process. They spend more and more time focusing attention on each other and less time with family and friends. The couple usually loses (for a time) some friends in the process, since quality fellowship is now substituted for passionate involvement. Relationships with natural parents, brothers and sisters - become more distant, since the couple are consumed with each other. As the emotions build, all they think about is each other and the next time they can be together, especially alone.

Step Five: Physical Involvement

Beginning with step three, and moving on at times through step four is the emotional attachment the couple begins to have. Its evidence is usually identified by simple actions such as standing closer and closer together, then holding hands, kissing and moving through other steps of sensual love which is really *lust* outside of marriage because it has selfish pleasure as its primary goal without the security of lifelong commitment.

The couple may have no idea the trap and web that is being laid for them. One's sexual desires are not designed to be started and stopped over and over again. God designed the process to begin and end as one unit and beautiful act of love that is a confirmation of the internal covenant and commitment already made before Him.

One's sexual desires are not designed to be utilized outside of God's moral boundary which is marriage. Thus, as sexual desires are spent, it is like a reserve tank being used for the wrong person at the wrong time. With little regard for the future, scars that will last a lifetime are built within the individual.

Step Six: Breaking Up - The Scar of Rejection

Since the main purpose of dating is to try out as many partners as possible in looking for the perfect one for you, breaking up is as common as dating itself. It is also the most painful part. More pop songs are recorded about the breaking up process than pairing up. The pain of losing someone's sensual love is a testimony of the attachment that is inherent in the moral laws God designed in relationships.

You see, we were designed to get sexually involved with only one person. Therefore, the pain in breaking up is, in seed form, the same as divorce, separation and having a marriage partner "cheat on you" with another individual. We are tied to that person physically and emotionally and thus the scar of rejection becomes a reality.

Physically we are torn apart and a scar forms, making us more callous and less giving in sexual love the next time. Why give more the next time when you got robbed this time - he just left! Yet the guilt of withholding love also drives the couple's sexual desires the next time. The girl invariably feels used. The guy forms his opinion of sexual love (even if he did not go "all the way") as a toy to be used at will. He rationalizes that it makes him more of a man. She forms a scar of frigidity (an inability to give physically in sexual love) and he forms a scar of callous lust that uses women for sport and pleasure.

Emotionally it is like being torn apart in your feelings. Thus, both partners become more callous in sharing emotions and feelings that are deep within. This is true later in life with those who have divorced or been separated for some reason. It is harder to give love the second time around. One needs the grace of God in order to overcome this, (and thank God that is possible) but God does not take away the consequences of our sin either. We pay a dear price for crossing God's boundaries. God allows us to live with the consequences of our actions so that we do not think there are no absolute boundaries. He also allows this for the benefit of others because we can help them prevent making our mistakes.

Spiritually, the conscience of both individuals is seared and becomes hardened to the things of God and His discernment. This primarily happens through the rejection caused by breaking up. As the conscience is hardened each time, there is less sensitivity until there is no conscience at all in relation to this area of life. As one dates many individuals, the boundaries and limits become faded and begin to disappear, and rejection becomes a way of life. What was once morally unacceptable becomes the norm, and the once beautiful flower of potential that was to bloom for one partner is ripped apart before it is really ready to blossom.

The Fruit of the Dating Process

One may argue at this point that it is possible to "date" without getting physically involved at all. The boy and girl are simply friends. They socialize together, learn to relate together, and never get passionately involved or emotionally attached. Thus, the potential for rejection is not as large or dangerous.

Cliff Hanging

The problem with this line of reasoning is that the dating pattern and relationship are still looked at as the best way to build social relationships. Of what good is it to simply reduce the pain of sinful consequences when they can be virtually eliminated? The goal of the Christian life is not to live on the edge of God's boundaries, seeing how far we can go without falling off! The goal is to see how high we can raise the standard for the sake of future generations and the impact it might have on advancing the Kingdom of God on earth.

The chances taken for temptation are much greater with couples than with natural teams in the family or church. The real issue that should be analyzed is whether one should take the risk or play it as safe as possible. Why develop a dangerous pattern of cliff-hanging, always in danger of falling off because one wishes to come as close to the edge as possible? One wrong move, or faulty decision, and your life is changed forever. Those who play it safe, as far from the edge as possible, have more room for failure without heavy consequences.

The real question should be: how far do you want to go in Christ?

> *"Can a man take fire in his bosom, and his clothes not be burned? Can one go upon hot coals, and his feet not be burned?"* - Proverbs 6:27-28

> *"Now the Spirit speaketh expressly, that in the latter times some shall depart from the faith, giving heed to seducing spirits, and doctrines of devils; speaking lies in hypocrisy; having their conscience seared with a hot iron; forbidding to marry..."* - I Timothy 4:1-3a

> *"... in the last days perilous times shall come. For men shall be lovers of their own selves, covetous.., unholy, without natural affection, truce breakers, incontinent..."* - II Timothy 3:1-3

Is it possible to follow the wrong pattern with a sincere heart and still reap the ill effects of it? Absolutely! What you sow you will reap. It is like putting fire in your clothes without thinking you will suffer burns - it doesn't happen. It is also like walking on hot coals and not thinking you will get burned. If you walk into a lion's den, you will suffer the consequences, regardless of how pure your motive may be. You may not be serious, but the lion is! You may think you are simply fooling around, but God's laws are still valid and your flesh will still operate negatively whether you like it or not.

What are the consequences? Well, for starters, we come into greater contact with demonic influence in our life as we veer away from God's boundaries. In other words, we become more like a puppet and less like an individual with a free will. Our conscience becomes seared and it is far more difficult to hear God.

According to the verses above, we can tend to love ourselves more than anyone; covet sexual fulfillment at all costs; become unholy, not understand true affection since we have a habit of fulfilling the wrong kind, and constantly have a habit of breaking covenants (breaking up, or truce breaking). We have also lost our self control (or we are incontinent.)

Unfulfilled Marriages

The pattern of being demonically oppressed with lustful thoughts, dreams and fantasies, laid while you were young, haunt you when you are married. You flirt with thoughts about other women or men, and fantasize about the dream marriage like you did when you were young. The pattern of going from one partner to another is repeated in dreams and temptations that become a way of life.

Your love of self makes you constantly frustrated as a wife, mother, husband or father whose priorities are wrong. Children, the greatest blessing of a marriage, become a nuisance that conflicts with careers and the "good life."

Since all you knew how to do was flirt and seduce, rather than respect and honor, you have a difficult time demonstrating true affection through simple manners. And, since all you knew how to do was flirt and seduce, you are devoid of respect and honor.

This all leads to an unfulfilled marriage. What is worse, you may pass this on to your own children who will repeat the same mistakes.

Adultery

Your loss of self-control has its consequences as well. As you flirt with thoughts, they become situations. These situations are recreated all the time. Scenes of temptation and falling into sin crowd your imagination as you try to sleep. Fear begins to grip you, because you wonder what you would do if the situations actually occurred. Due to the first consequence, your lack of fulfillment leads only to more dreams and fantasies, until you are set up for a temptation and potential fall into adultery. Ask anyone who is willing to share with you their failings in this area; it always begins with patterns in youth and the teen years, only to bear fruit later on.

Divorce

However, at the heart of the dating process is covenant-breaking. We learn to break covenants at whim when we feel like it or when our emotions need some uplifting. The entire dating process is like entering covenants from the backdoor. The fact of pairing up is a covenant. When you get involved physically or even emotionally before you are ready for marriage then you form a covenant that probably will not hold you since it was not born internally in the heart of God.

Covenant breaking is a thought process that says that if it doesn't work out, you can simply break it off instead of working it out. It takes maturity and experience to work things out. That is why the forming of relationships with those who do not pose as much of a temptation emotionally ought to be pursued for the real practice of handling true friendship.

The dating commitment is shallow because it is built on feeling. A relationship begun on emotional or sensual feeling will only last as long as the feelings last. Then, there is no reason to continue. This results in a pattern of divorce. It is practicing for divorce at an early age. Ask anyone who has lived through one; *divorce is death*. It is the death of a covenant that is almost unbearable, no matter what you think of the partner. It is more devastating upon the children within the marriage who must learn by experience the devastation of sinful covenant breaking.

Thus, what are the results of the dating process? Does it help prepare us for restoring the generations and rebuilding the walls against the enemy? Certainly not, for it only produces more gaping holes and scars that are with us for life. It prepares us for unfulfilled marriages, adultery and divorce.

Now this does not mean that if you have committed adultery or been a part of a divorce situation it is *only* because of your pattern of dating. Neither does this mean that those who date *automatically* will commit adultery in the future or get a divorce. However, the potential for these things is greatly increased if you sow the wrong seed while young. It brings hindrances to fulfilled marriages and causes great delays in fulfilling God's call upon your life. No wonder our nation is in the state it is in today!

God help us as a joint generation of teens and adults to act as a jury, and upon examining the evidence, to place an indictment of "GUILTY" upon this process of dating and all of its sensual habits. We must seek a better way.

Religious Sensuality

You may have picked it up while reading, but let me make it clear here that there is also no place for "Christian dating" or the religious candy-coating of the same sinful process. Just because two individuals are Christians does not in any way insure against the same devastating results. We cannot "Christianize" the dating process, we must eradicate it. It is not just the fact of dating that is detrimental to our preparation of fulfilling God's call. It is the process of attachment.

Even if you knew you were going to marry the one you were dating, the process would not prepare you properly for marriage since it is built upon the wrong foundation.

There is no sense in adopting "religious sensuality" as the deceptive replacement for dating. It is sin whether conducted within the church or on the street corner. Having devotions before or after your sensual date does not sanctify it. Embracing a "ministry" where a guy endeavors to convert his date is sheer madness. These are all shallow excuses for foolish endeavors. In fact, they are lies. God does not lead individuals into ministries that break His principles or sidestep His moral walls.

Dating vs. Courtship

Let us be honest. The dating process needs to be replaced! The evidence of the need to replace the dating process is often verified by the fact that we know of no other way to get married! We have become ignorant of God's ways, and all we are left with are the ways of the world. That is all we have known.

However, if the dating pattern is not Biblical, reasonable or successful, then even common sense causes us to look for a remedy. The best place to begin is with a Biblical understanding of marriage and sex. We must start at the beginning and work our way toward replacing man's tradition of failure with God's law of success.

Lesson Three

A BIBLICAL VIEW
OF MARRIAGE AND SEX

We need to discuss marriage before sex. This is simply because God has ordained sexual endeavors to be within the boundaries of the marriage relationship. Often we have a false view of dating, sex, and related topics because we do not have a correct view about marriage.

> *"So God created man in his own image, in the image of God created he him; male and female created he them. And God blessed them, and God said unto them, Be fruitful, and multiply, and replenish the earth, and subdue it; and have dominion..."* - Genesis 1:27-28

> *"And Adam said, this is now bone of my bones, and flesh of my flesh; she shall be called Woman, because she was taken out of Man. Therefore, shall a man leave his father and his mother, and shall cleave unto his wife; and they shall be one flesh. And they were both naked, the man and his wife, and were not ashamed."* - Genesis 2:23-25

When God created man (male and female) He did so with a purpose. Although they were distinct individuals with different personalities and physical make-ups, Adam and Eve had a destiny, a calling and a purpose for which God created them. They were not created simply for their own pleasure. Their first purpose together was to bear the image of God. Thus, their primary purpose was toward God, to get to know Him. Secondarily, they were to be fruitful and multiply (have children), replenish the earth (creatively use their talents and liberty,) and subdue or take dominion of the earth (be good stewards over the property they used.) This call we often refer to as

God's dominion mandate; the respect for life (children), liberty (creativity,) and property (ownership of land.)

How would mankind fulfill such a lofty calling? The method God would use to bring children into the world would be *marriage*. The training children would receive would release their gifts and talents through the discipline of their sinful nature, in order to prepare them for stewardship of the earth in fulfilling God's call. Thus, sex had its primary purpose within marriage as *procreation*.

The marriage relationship had three parts to it that we can discern from Genesis, chapter two:

1. The act of **leaving** referred to man's spiritual nature. Men and women are spiritual in nature, relating to moral and spiritual principles that lift one above mere existence on the earth. Marriage is the spiritual foundation of a new generation. Leaving your father and mother implies an end to the old relationship and the beginning of a new family. Old things are passing away, and all things are becoming new.

2. The act of **cleaving** referred to man's social nature. Men and women are social by nature and enjoy companions. Marriage and the home are the social foundations for society. Relationships are here demonstrated, nurtured and practiced. In the context of the home and marriage, the discipline of forming lasting relationships is established.

3. The act of becoming **one flesh** referred to man's physical nature. Men and women are also physical in nature. We have physical desires, and our bodies were created in such a way as to be drawn together as male and female in sexual union.

However, the order is clear. We must first have the spiritual calling to leave, and the commitment to cleave before we can be of one flesh with another. Outside of this, we break God's laws and boundaries and will suffer the consequences.

35

God's First Purpose for Marriage
(A Picture of Christ and the Church)

"And God said, Let us make man in our image, after our likeness... " - Genesis 1:26a

"And the rib, which the Lord God had taken from man, made he a woman, and brought her unto the man." - Genesis 2:22

"For we are members of his body, of his flesh, and of his bones. For this cause shall a man leave his father and mother, and shall be joined unto his wife, and they two shall be one flesh. This is a great mystery, but I speak concerning Christ and the church."
- Ephesians 5:30-31

God's first purpose for marriage was to demonstrate to the world the relationship He desired between Himself and mankind. God desired to create man, unlike the animals, after His own kind so that he was made in His image. In this way, God could have intimate communion and fellowship with His highest creation - mankind. That is why He created Eve out of the side of Adam - to demonstrate this picture.

When mankind fell into sin, God had to send a substitute (Jesus Christ) to the earth to die in his place. Then, man could once again have a close relationship with God. Jesus became the head of the church, which is Christ's body. The church is also called the Bride of Christ. God desires to demonstrate to all nations that He wants to marry His church one day. The church must be cleansed, purified and ready to be the wife of the Lord Jesus. In a sense, this is the task of the Holy Spirit.

The marriage relationship is a testimony of how God desires to have a close relationship with all peoples on the earth. Thus, marriage has a higher meaning than simply personal pleasure, security or happiness. It is ultimately a great mystery that God desires to have demonstrated now and that will one day, at Christ's return, be a reality.

Sexual union also has this high purpose. It demonstrates the kind of close, intimate union God wants with mankind. The verb used in the Bible for the phrase "to know God" is also used for sexual union.

The pleasure of knowing God, who meets your every need through love, is true spiritual reality. That is why God created sexual union with such fulfillment and pleasure. It is a physical demonstration of a major spiritual truth. God is not against pleasure or fulfilling your desires. However, He knows what is best for us, and that is why He builds clear walls and moral boundaries for its proper use. Sexual union has primarily a spiritual purpose to demonstrate one's need for intimacy with a loving God.

God's Second Purpose for Marriage
(To Fulfill His Plan and Purpose in the Earth)

"And God blessed Noah and his sons, and said unto them; Be fruitful, and multiply, and replenish the earth." - Genesis 9:1

After the flood, God repeated to Noah and his sons the original purpose for which He created mankind, *the dominion mandate*. This was indeed a new beginning, or a foundation for new generations after the great Flood. God's plan of marriage, which we just considered, became the method through which God would fulfill His purposes.

Through marriage, God would bring forth new life upon the earth (be fruitful and multiply). This would fill the earth with people who were to continue to fulfill His purposes. Succeeding generations would then continue to fulfill His plan. God wanted the earth reformed creatively (or replenished) through the diligence and work of man. From electricity to satellites and spaceships, man has since taken the materials in the earth, discovered the laws built into creation, and reformed these materials into various creative expressions. Finally, God desired for man to be a steward over the property of the earth (to subdue) in governing it with Him.

Thus, it should not come as a shock or surprise to have Satan come and attack God's plan in this very area of marriage. In Genesis, chapter three, Satan tried to break down Eve's relationship with her husband and both of their relationships with God by planting seeds of disrespect, mistrust and doubt. In this way, he could make a hole in the foundation and thus get part of the offspring to do what he wanted. When marriage and the home are destroyed, sexual immorality follows, for sexual fulfillment always occurs within the boundaries of marriage.

We need to recapture today God's ultimate purpose for marriage: first, to be a declaration of the image of God and second, to be a channel of blessing to generations which follow to fulfill God's plan on the earth. This will be done by renewing God's picture as a testimony of His relationship to man - solid marriages - and also to accomplish His will through children brought up in such a way as to embrace God's vision for multi-generations.

Contrasting Views on Marriage and Sex

After this introduction on God's purpose for marriage and sex, let us contrast the views of the Bible with those commonly taught today. The chart that follows compares what God says about marriage and sex with the way the world sees marriage and sex today. This chart can be an excellent place to start in discussing these topics with parents and teens. Or, if you are a single adult, with other individuals of the same sex as you ponder the values and attitudes you wish to adopt in your life in preparation for whatever God may have for you.

The Word of God	The World Today
Marriage has eternal meaning, being a picture of Christ and His church - God's ultimate purpose for creating mankind (Ephesians 5:22-23)	Marriage has temporal meaning, merely a partnership to help each fulfill their own desires & careers.
Sex is spiritual as well as physical, and is the result of an internal covenant within marriage (Genesis 2:24)	Sex is only physical, and its only limit is the choice of the two or more individuals involved.

38

The destruction of the marriage relationship through adultery or other perversions leads to the destruction of society as well, (Deuteronomy 28:15-18)

Old fashioned ideas about marriage inflict unneeded restraints upon people and tend to produce guilt and shame when there is no need.

Sex is perverted outside of heterosexual marriage, causing spiritual judgment. (Heb. 13:8)

Sexual preference is a free choice of individuals, and should have no dictates from any institution or authority.

Marriage involves a covenant commitment for life that builds security in long term relationships, balancing pleasure with responsibility (Mt. 19:3-9)

Marriage is a joint agreement so long as both want it. It should be easily entered and easily dissolved. Its purpose is for one's own pleasure.

Sex involves both pleasure and responsibility. It takes Godly motives and knowledge in order to give and please the other (1st Cor. 7:3-5)

Sex involves pleasure only and is legitimate when one's motive is simply to get some pleasure. Getting satisfaction is one of the reasons for being sexually active.

Committing sin that destroys the marriage relationship is serious in the eyes of God and causes judgment (1st Cor. 6:9-11)

There are no consequences to extramarital relationships other than what affects you or your mate. One needs to play his cards right.

Sex outside of God's boundaries causes you to sin and judge your own body, thus destroying God's temple (1st Cor. 6:15-20)

People who suffer diseases from sexual acivity are victims - all of us should seek to have safe sexual activity without consequences.

Waiting for the right person to marry is essential so that you are equally yoked and joined together by God (Mark 10:9)

Living together and enjoying one another lets you try many individuals out and reduce the risk of a lifelong commitment.

Keeping yourself pure before marriage is an honor before God and before your marriage partner. (1st Timothy 4:12; 5:2)	Virginity is out - sexual freedom is in. Virginity is a sign of old fashioned ideas no longer valid in a society free from moral absolutes.
Adultery, fornication, and sexual impurity include impure attitudes and not just the act of sexual intercourse (Mt. 5:28-30)	Adultery and fornication only involve the actual act of intercourse - and due to disease or risk, it may be wise to protect yourself with birth control or abstinence.
The best way to prepare for marriage is to reserve all sexual passion for one mate; since the physical is the seal of the spiritual and social aspects of marriage (1st Cor. 7:1-2)	The best way to prepare for marriage (if that is what you want) is to be sexually active with as many individuals as possible before settling down with one; and then, there is always divorce.

Biblical Sex Education

"All things are lawful unto me, but all things are not expedient; all things are lawful for me, but I will not be brought under the power of any.... Now the body is not for fornication, but for the Lord; and the Lord for the body." - 1 Corinthians 6:12-13

Our physical bodies are not inherently evil. Talking about sexual matters and biological facts about our bodies should be healthy, and should not make us ashamed to speak with our parents (as if the topic was a secret). Asceticism, or the putting of our bodies down as part of the earth and therefore not of God, is against the very principles of Christianity. The earth is the Lord's, as well as everything that He created on it, which includes our bodies (Psalm 24:1).

However, God here declares that we should not be brought under the power of the body. We are to have our body as our servant, not our master. This is part of learning to live under the Lordship of Jesus Christ. Our body is to carry out God's will as we yield to Him in our spirit and soul. The body is not for fornication; it is for the Lord. We are to yield it to Him as a reasonable part of our service.

God is also for the body! The Lord is for your body. He created it, and desires for it to function as He created it to function. Thus, the natural sex hormones which He created within your body are natural and God-given. They are not evil. God is for the body and all of its created functions, including sex! It was God's idea in the first place. However, He desires that you willingly and voluntarily control and govern these functions so that they are released within His boundaries and moral laws for your best good and to fulfill His highest plan for the Kingdom of God.

Hormones are formed from your blood, and secreted by ductless glands within your body. Organs, such as your thyroid, para thyroid, pituitary gland, adrenal gland and pancreas, secrete hormones all the time which influence your neck, throat, brain, strength and other such activities. In addition to these types of hormones, everyone has sexual hormones as well.

God created each individual to have both primary and secondary sexual characteristics. The primary characteristics are quite obvious and include all of the sex organs and body parts. It is important that each individual know how he or she is made and what the function of each part is, with its proper biological name. Any biology text or encyclopedia can be a source to study the reproductive process and corresponding body parts.

God also created each individual with secondary sexual characteristics which include the operation of sex hormones secreted by the ovaries in the female and the testes in the male. You may remember that one of the functions of the ovaries in the female is to produce eggs that can be fertilized in the conception process, which is what makes a woman pregnant. The testes in the male produce sperm cells which fertilize the egg in the woman.

However, the ovaries and testes do more than function in the reproductive process. They also secrete hormones which arouse both males and females sexually. These hormones, testosterone in the male, and estrogen in the female, cause one to go through puberty (physical maturation of the primary sexual characteristics and body parts) at about age 11 or 12 and form the basis of the sex drive in your physical body. These hormones are aroused in different ways for men and women.

> *"For this is the will of God, even your sanctification, that ye should abstain from fornication: that everyone of you should know how to possess his vessel in sanctification and honor; not in the lust of concupiscence (sexual impurity), even as the Gentiles which know not God; that no man go beyond and defraud (take advantage of) his brother in any matter; because that the Lord is the avenger of all such, as we also have forewarned you and testified."*
> - I Thessalonians 4:3-6

If we are stimulated with thoughts or actions that are sexually attractive, our bodies react powerfully through the secretion of the hormones mentioned earlier. God desires each of us to be good stewards over our bodies so that we do not abuse the sexual drive that is part of our physical nature. Part of stewardship, as we have seen, is preserving that which God intended for marriage until that time.

God does not wish for us to use the opportunities we have in our relationships with each other to take advantage of another's weakness. This means that if we, as brothers and sisters in Christ, tempt each other by the way we dress, walk, talk, or look at each other, we are defrauding one another. God says in strong language that He will judge (or avenge) the individuals involved in this. Often, beginning in spiritual contexts and true ministry, our physical bodies take over and what began in ministry ends in sexual temptation and lustful thinking. That is why it is important for us to erect walls and fences so that we can protect one another rather than defraud one another.

The physical natures of men and women are different. That is why God says that we are to dwell together in marriage "with knowledge" (I Peter 3:7,) understanding how different we are as men and women. Just as God instructs husbands and wives to watch over each other's bodies as part of their own property (I Corinthians 7:3-5 and Ephesians 5:28-29,) we need to do the same in preparation now.

We need to be cautious that we do not in any way become a stumbling block to our brothers and sisters. More will be said about this later, but it is important to simply recognize the following in relation to the differences between men and women physically and how they are aroused sexually.

The Physical Nature of Men

A man's sexual hormones are aroused quickly by sight. All a man needs to see, in a sense, is a suggestive picture and his hormones kick into gear! That is why the advertising industry uses women who are suggestively dressed and walk seductively to sell cars, hairspray or just about anything they wish to sell to men. Our society has become addicted to defrauding one another in this way. It should make every young lady angry to see the way her body is flaunted and used as bait for materialistic pleasures!

Physical passion is an engine in all of us that begins to build if we allow it to do so. Within marriage, it is a special time of intimacy to express unconditional love. Outside of marriage, it must be restrained so that it can be expressed at the right time once married. In men, it builds quickly and moves from low to high in a matter of minutes. Thus, if a man's sexual hormones are turned on through sight, it does not take long for him to put into action what his body is dictating unless he consciously governs his own physical nature, which he is capable of doing.

That is why many police detectives have found that upon investigating crimes of rape, sexual murder and other gross perversions, pornographic pictures were involved. How can a picture cause such violent crimes? It is because of the nature of men in a physical sense; they are turned on by sight, and their passion goes from low to high in a very short time frame if not carefully governed. When a man has lived his life without restraint in this area, his physical body becomes the master and lust takes over quickly, bringing forth violent behavior.

Men also go from high to low in a matter of minutes. That is why it is easier for a man to simply walk away, leaving a woman pregnant or even raping her. His emotions are not as involved, and once his sex drive is lowered, he is indifferent and even detached from what happened. This is also why more men desert women more than women desert men. It is easier to leave the situation, even if others are hurt. Men do not often notice feelings or atmosphere to the degree that women do.

Women must understand these things in order to act properly. Women must be careful how they dress. What a woman may feel is a modest dress, for instance, may not be modest at all if you are considering the men in the room. Colors, tightness of fit, length and which part of the body is exposed have a lot to do with the matter. If we really love one another we will not want to defraud (take advantage of) each other, and thus we will protect one another by the way that we look and act. In this way, our knowledge about one another will help us to preserve each other's purity.

Women must also learn not to set themselves up for rejection and hurt because they are simply ignorant of a man's nature. If a guy is making suggestive advances upon a girl, or if he is just being friendly, she should protect herself and not allow the first step of flattery to take hold upon her. What was meant as simple friendship in a guy can easily be taken as emotional attachment in a girl. She must realize that it would be nothing for him, normally, (whether intentional or not) to lift her emotions, send her into fantasy land, and then pay closer attention to another girl who happens to be dressed more sensually at the moment. This has caused girls (and women) who are desperate for attention to dress as immodestly as possible - with an intent upon getting the man's physical passion stirred.

We should be protecting each other rather than defrauding each other. On the positive side, if a man governs his sexual drive and keeps it under control, his physical make-up can be an asset. The reason God made men and their adrenaline to move so quickly is to be the leader and protector in danger and other situations. A man can react quickly, and bring protection, even before a woman knows she is in trouble. Our goal should be to cultivate the positive aspects of a man's nature

44

now so that we learn to govern ourselves and not be in bondage to our physical bodies.

The Physical Nature of Women

Women are very different from men. They are not aroused as much by sight; their hormones are aroused more by feeling, emotion, atmosphere and touch. That is why advertising agencies, when they wish to sell something to women, present an atmosphere and music of emotion and feeling rather than simply showing a man half-dressed, (though due to our present culture, arousal by sight is now becoming more common place in both men and women). This ignites a woman's hormones more prevalently than visual sight.

A woman's passion is also very different. She moves from low to high in her sex drive more slowly. She gets involved deeply. Her emotions are taken and her feelings are deeply involved. It takes time to get her "ready" for physical involvement. That is why it is usually the guys who force sex on a date (date-rape as we saw it labeled). The girls are not as ready so quickly. However, they are the ones deeply hurt and rejected as well. Thus, women need to protect themselves and recognize their own weaknesses.

Men must recognize that "friendliness" can often turn into "leading on" someone suggestively. It is all in the motive. A young lady can tell instantly whether someone is opening a door due to courteous attention or due to suggestive intentions. A man's motive is clearly seen by the woman because she senses atmosphere and feels something that men often are not even aware of. The men must protect the women's emotions and provide protection, as men are called to lead in this way.

Men should stay out of any "tempting environment" in order to protect the women. Being alone at night, in a bedroom, or any other similar type of environment is only asking for trouble. It is not fair to the girl or woman because it is setting her up for defrauding. We abuse true love and friendship when we treat each other this way. Staying in groups, with the lights on, and keeping motives pure, will go a long way toward protecting what God desires to cultivate in men and women.

On the positive side, women are often tremendous in discerning the motive and atmosphere of a situation. They ponder and do not react quickly. This is an asset as a woman learns to govern her physical nature and utilize her strengths for positive spiritual leadership. Women can usually sense a problem in advance through pondering a situation, and are usually more committed in the long-term than a man as he grows up. Let us keep these positive characteristics at the forefront of our motives and actions so that as a team we can work together!

Flee Fornication

"Flee fornication. Every sin that a man doeth is without the body; but he that committeth fornication sinneth against his own body." - I Corinthians 6:18

"Now concerning the things whereof ye wrote unto me; it is good for a man not to touch (arouse the passion of) a woman." - I Corinthians 7:1

God built moral boundaries and laws within our physical bodies. In other words, if you violate the moral laws of God, your bodies will respond accordingly with sickness and even death. Often, the way the judgment of God is expressed is not the same with different people, but be sure that your sin will find you out (see Numbers 32:23). Fornication is a sin against your own body. God says we are to *flee* fornication. Many feel this simply means refraining from the act of sexual intercourse. But from a Biblical context, it means to stay as far away as possible from the entire process! Do not even go close to it. After all, that is what fleeing is all about!

It is important to recognize just what fornication really is, and so the chart that closes out this chapter is for that purpose. The Bible says that we should understand the traps and snares that await us, and in this way plan not to fall into them (Proverbs 22:3; Romans 13:14).

The word "fornication" comes from the Greek "porneia," from which we get pornography. It is a broad term which can include homosexuality, adultery, beastiality or any attitude that leads up to these. It is important to distinguish between internal fornication and external fornication. One is a matter of the heart and mind, and the other an act. Jesus gave the scope and meaning of fornication when He stated:

> *"Ye have heard that it was said by them of old time, thou shalt not commit adultery; but I say unto you, that whosoever looketh on a woman to lust after her hath committed adultery with her already in his heart."* - Matthew 5:27-28

Thus, Jesus taught that adultery, or fornication, begins in the heart. The entire process, from heart inclination to deed, should be avoided. As the Apostle Paul put it in I Corinthians 7:1, it is better for a man not to touch a woman. The word touch means to "light the fires of passion" within a woman. Thus, it is better for a man never to arouse passion in a woman that is not his wife. It is also good for women not to arouse the passion of men through the way they dress, walk and act as well. We need to place the boundary right where God places it - the fence needs to be built far enough away from the cliff for the purpose of remaining pure and fulfilling God's plan in our lives.

To play with temptation through immodesty or sensuality, is to neglect the most practical meaning of the word "flee". If you run away from something, you do not hang around and play with that which could harm you. You flee! Thus, every believer's attitude toward arousing sexual passion (in a deliberate way) in another before marriage (fornication) or with someone other than your marriage partner (adultery) ought to be staying as far away from the process as possible!

Within marriage, the chart on page 43 would have its positive fulfillment in love and not in deceptive and subtle lust. One desires to give, and the other desires to receive. Outside of marriage, the entire process (as charted) needs to be avoided. Let us expose the entire fornication process, from thought to deed. The words defined below and the chart that follows involves the fornication (or adultery) process outside of its proper marital boundaries.

Definition of Biblical Terms

The following definitions from Webster's 1828 Dictionary[2] and Strong's Concordance[3] will help you to see how the Bible classifies the sexual conduct of individuals (most of the words used for sexual activity outside of marriage). Note how the words include both internal attitudes and external actions.

Let God's standard of righteousness be revealed in the etymology of the words most often used for purity and impurity in the Bible. The King James Version is used here because of the clarity of the words and the clear definitions they reveal.

Adultery - "violation of the marriage bed; unfaithfulness of any married person to the marriage bed" - from the Greek - *moichos* - "apostate, a male paramour (lover)".

Chaste - "pure from all unlawful commerce of sexes. Free of obscenity; pure; genuine; uncorrupt; free from barbarous words and phrases, and from quaint, affected, extravagant expressions. - from the Greek - *hagnon* - "clean, innocent, modest, perfect, pure".

Concupiscence - "lust; unlawful or irregular desire of sexual pleasure..; inclination for unlawful enjoyments." - from the Greek - *epithunzia* - "a longing (for what is forbidden), desire, lust."

Incontinency - "want of restraint of the sexual appetite; free or illegal indulgence of lust; lewdness; used of either sex, but appropriately of the male sex; unchaste." - from the Greek - *akrasia* - "want of self-restraint, excess, powerless, without self-control."

Lasciviousness - "looseness; irregular indulgence of animal desires; wantonness; lustfulness. Tendency to excite lust, and promote irregular

---

[2] Noah Webster's first edition of *An American Dictionary of the English Language*, 1828; facsimile edition published by the Foundation for American Christian Education, San Francisco, California, 1967.

[3] James Strong, *The Exhaustive Concordance of the Bible*, MacDonald Publishing Co., McLean, Virginia.

indulgences." - from the Greek - *aselgeia* - "licentiousness, filthy, wantonness."

Lewdness - "the unlawful indulgence of lust; fornication, or adultery, idolatry, licentiousness; shamelessness." - from the Greek - *rhadiourgema* - "reckless, easygoing behavior."

Lust - "a burning, longing desire; carnal appetite; depraved affections and desires; (lustful) provoking to sensuality; inciting to lust or exciting carnal desire." - from the Greek - *epithumia* - (same as above).

Temptation - "solicitation of the passions; enticements to evil proceeding from the prospect of pleasure or advantage." - from the Greek - *peirasmos* - "a test, attempt, adversity, proof".

Virgin - "a woman who has had no carnal knowledge of man, pure, untouched, as virgin gold; fresh, new, unused, etc." - from the Greek - *parthenos* - "maiden, unmarried daughter."

Wantonness - "sportiveness; gayety; frolicksomeness; licentiousness; negligence of restraint. (wanton) "wandering or roving in gayety or sport; darting aside, or one way and the other, moving or flying loosely; wandering from moral rectitude; dissolute; indulging in sensuality without restraint; deviating from the rules of chastity; lewd; lustful; lascivious." from the Greek - *aselgeia* - (same as above).

Whoredom - "lewdness; fornication; practice of unlawful commerce with the other sex. It is applied to either sex, and to any kind of illicit commerce." (whore) - "a harlot; a prostitute." - from the Greek - *pernos* - "a male prostitute."

A chart utilizing many of these words in the process of fornication or adultery is given on the next page. Keep in mind that the chart illustrates the areas of involvement and terminology of the entire process of sexual involvement *outside of marriage.* An open and loving relationship, under the protection of covenantal commitment, would have different words describing differing attitudes involved, since it would be the positive expression of love within a marital setting. This chart exposes that from which we ought to flee!

In our next lesson we will focus on how we can cultivate our hearts to obey God and avoid the trap of sexual impurity.

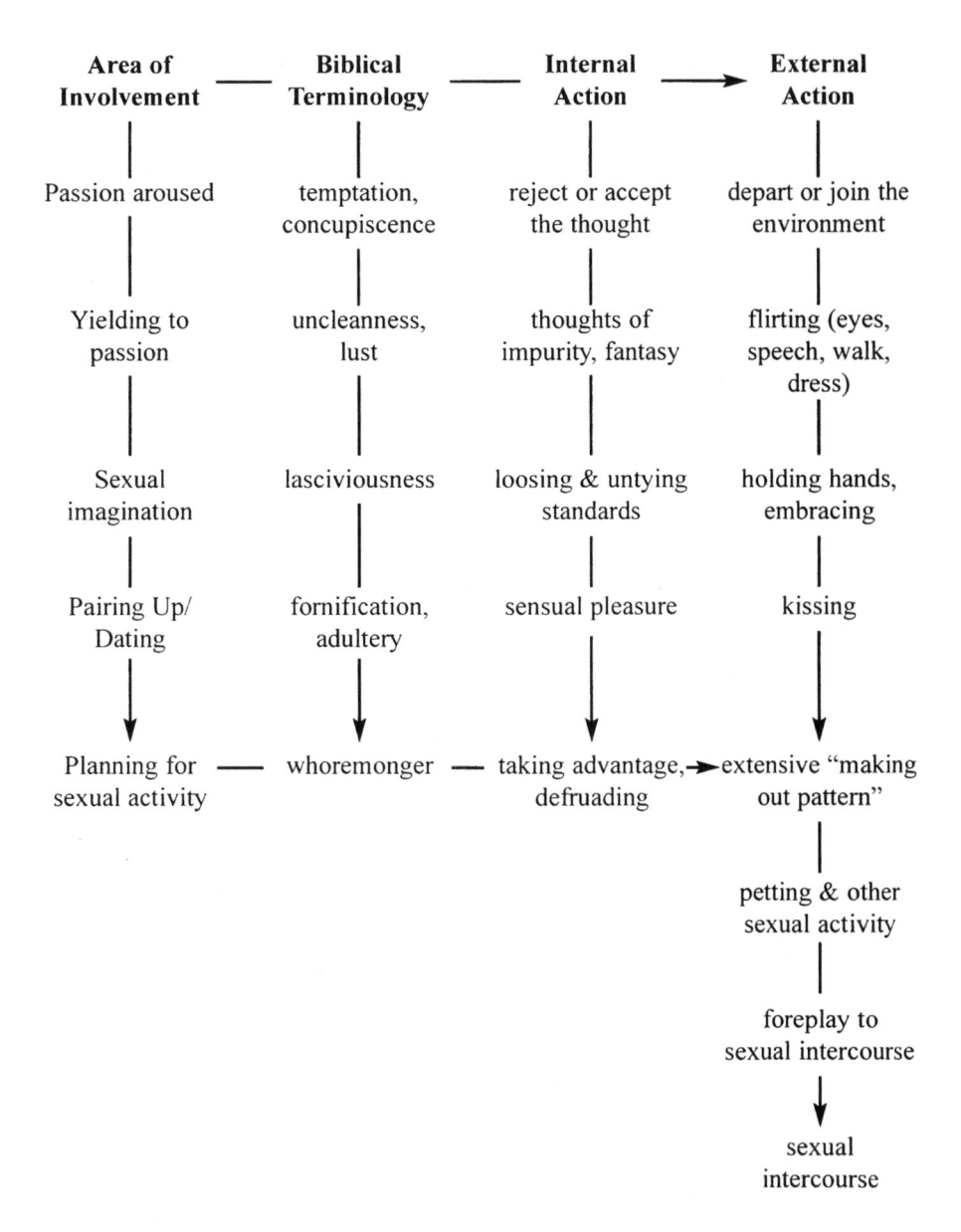

Area of Involvement	Biblical Terminology	Internal Action	External Action
Passion aroused	temptation, concupiscence	reject or accept the thought	depart or join the environment
Yielding to passion	uncleanness, lust	thoughts of impurity, fantasy	flirting (eyes, speech, walk, dress)
Sexual imagination	lasciviousness	loosing & untying standards	holding hands, embracing
Pairing Up/ Dating	fornification, adultery	sensual pleasure	kissing
Planning for sexual activity	whoremonger	taking advantage, defruading	extensive "making out pattern"
			petting & other sexual activity
			foreplay to sexual intercourse
			sexual intercourse

Lesson Four

CULTIVATING A
PURE HEART BEFORE GOD

Virginity, as we saw in the last lesson, means "pure," "new" and "unused," and refers literally to one who has had no sexual intercourse before marriage. If we take into consideration the teachings of Jesus, we must conclude that virginity has both an internal and external meaning, just as fornication does. To refer to virginity only as "waiting until marriage," implying that the final act is the only thing that is reserved, we tend to look at virginity in only an external manner. One can be a virgin externally; but in thought and habitual thinking, not a virgin at all. Total or complete virginity should then include both internal and external aspects of purity - spirit (or heart,) soul (or mind,) and body.

Internal virginity deals with internal purity and whether one's emotions, passions and thought life are pure before God. This involves the heart. It is important for us to begin here. If one's heart is not cultivated in purity before the Lord, it will be difficult, if not impossible, to keep one's external life free from impurity as well. The Bible tells us that the degree to which we keep our heart is the degree to which our external life is kept pure and holy as well (see Proverbs 4:23).

External virginity deals with external purity in sexual relations before marriage. Once this is lost, it can never be regained. It is the culmination and result of a pure lifestyle before God and man. There are definite advantages to retaining one's physical virginity before marriage. Although internal virginity, or the heart attitude, can be regained through the blood and forgiveness of the Lord and changing one's habits of thinking (though the consequences of spending passion will still be with us,) the results of losing one's external virginity can be more devastating physically, emotionally and spiritually.

51

Virginity (both internal and external) is the inheritance that you bring with you into marriage. When you bring total purity, you bring habits of self-denial and selfless giving into your marriage, and you have stored energy and passion that will help your marriage start on a stronger foundation. You will also have more to give to others. This is very important. This will enable you to get a "head start," in a sense, and surpass what your parents or other adults could do in their own lives, thus fulfilling God's call to the generations.

Let us examine the law of God with respect to virginity so we can see God's righteous standard for our lives:

> *"If any man take a wife, and go in unto her, and hate her, and give occasions of speech against her, and bring up an evil name upon her, and say, I took this woman, and when I came to her, I found her not a maid."* - Deuteronomy 22:13-14

1. The first law we will call God's <u>Standard</u> <u>of Virginity</u>.

It was expected for all unmarried women to be virgins. It was the accepted practice in Israel and anything less was considered sin and helping to destroy the society of the Hebrew nation. Thus, we can see that today in our society, and around the world, since the expected standard is a *loss* of virginity, the nations suffer under God's judgment as a consequence.

> *"... then shall the father of the damsel, and her mother, take and bring forth the tokens of the damsel's virginity unto the elders of the city in the gate; and the damsel's father shall say unto the elders, I gave my daughter unto this man to wife, and he hateth her; and lo, he hath given occasions of speech against her, saying, I found not thy daughter a maid; and yet these are the tokens of my daughter's virginity. And they shall spread the cloth before the elders of the city. And the elders of that city shall take that man and chastise him;*

shall amerce him in an hundred shekels of silver, and give them unto the father of the damsel, because he hath brought up an evil name upon a virgin of Israel; and she shall be his wife; he may not put her away all his days." - Deuteronomy 22:15-19

2. The second law we will call a <u>Virgin's</u> <u>Protection</u>.

God gave the father of the home the responsibility for protecting a daughter's virginity. It was his job to defend his daughter's reputation, as we see in the above passage. In fact, he and his wife were to provide the proof of their daughter's virginity.[4] The husband who accused her was punished and could not divorce her for any reason.

"But if this thing be true, and the tokens of virginity be not found for the damsel; then they shall bring out the damsel to the door of her father's house, and the men of her city shall stone her with stones that she die; because she hath wrought folly in Israel, to play the whore in her father's house; so shalt thou put evil away from among you." - Deuteronomy 22:20-21

3. The third law we will call the <u>Right</u> <u>of Virginity</u>.

In God's Law, a man had a right to find a girl a virgin if she said she was. Again this shows the high degree to which God looked upon virginity. If the husband found out that she had lied deliberately, and was a whore (prostitute) instead of a virgin girl, she was stoned to death. Thus, the sin of prostitution was severely punished.

---

[4] The sheet spread out in front of the elders by the parents is the bed sheet from the first night of marriage. A virgin girl has a thin layer of skin called the hymen which breaks during sexual intercourse. In the Bible, the blood on the sheet is called the "proof of her virginity". With increased athletic activity in women today, it is possible that this membrance may break before marriage without one being sexually active.

"If a man find a damsel that is a virgin which is not betrothed, and lay hold on her, and lie with her, and they be found; then the man that lay with her shall give unto the damsel's father fifty shekels of silver, and she shall be his wife, because he hath humbled her, he may not put her away all his days." -Deuteronomy 22:28-29

4. A fourth law from God is the <u>Responsibility</u> of <u>Marriage</u>.

If a single man and woman have sexual intercourse outside of marriage, then they have a responsibility to immediately consider marriage. This is because their sexual union is a covenant before God (see I Corinthians 6:15-17.) If they do not get married due to the girl's wishes (the father spoke for her daughter) refusing to marry because of an unequally yoked marriage, then the man still owes the woman a dowry (we will discuss this more fully in Lesson Seven) as if he married her (see Exodus 22:16-17.)

In other words, he still has financial responsibility as if he had married her. Keeping one's virginity avoids such potentially forced marriages. When couples who are even seriously considering marriage do not govern their sexual appetites, they may find themselves forced to have hurry-up weddings and quick marriages. This removes the objective discernment to understand whether God is really drawing the couple together, for everything is now focused on the fact that they have actually become "one" ahead of time.

"When a man hath taken a wife, and married her, and it come to pass that she find no favor in his eyes, because he hath found some uncleanness in her; then let him write her a bill of divorcement, and give it in her hand, and send her out of his house."
- Deuteronomy 24:1

5. A fifth law on virginity involves the potential for <u>Divorce</u>.

Divorce is the death of a marriage. It occurs internally long before it occurs externally. Here it is stated that if a man does not find his wife to be a virgin upon marrying her, or he finds that she does not continue to be faithful to the marriage covenant, he has the legitimate right to divorce her. This is what is called the "exception clause" in the Bible, or what many refer to as the only legitimate reason for divorce today - *unfaithfulness to the marriage covenant,* or the committing of adultery. The point to emphasize here, however, is the fact that loss of virginity before marriage tends to produce a pattern for potential unfaithfulness during marriage, which greatly increases the risk of divorce. Why pronounce a death sentence upon marriage before one even gets married?

Upon reading these laws from God's Word, one might think that love played no part in all of this. It seems so cold and matter-of-fact. However, we must take into consideration what Jesus did when He taught in the New Testament. Jesus made it clear to the Pharisees and others that it was not only a matter of "law" but also the heart.

That is what we are primarily dealing with in this lesson. We need to see the righteous standard of God's Law, but we must also recognize that Jesus made it a matter of the heart. No individual should ever look for a reason or excuse to divorce his wife, for instance, for God never meant it to be a solution for a difficult marriage (see Matthew 19:1-12). Reconciliation and healing, as well as forgiveness for any sin committed prior to or during marriage should be our primary response and goal. Jesus increased the emphasis of the Law to include the heart attitude, and therefore, it was more difficult to adhere to God's Law than simply obeying the *letter* rather than the *spirit.*

However, we must realize that there are still consequences for our actions. For instance, a very high percentage of marriages brought together after loss of virginity end in divorce (some statistics report up to 80%). That is why God did not allow forced marriages to divorce. The only clause in God's law that *allows* divorce is the unfaithfulness of the marriage partner in adultery or fornication. God may allow this in His Law, but He *hates divorce* (see Malachi 2:16.)

Both partners in a forced marriage (they marry because they have had sexual relations) have already committed fornication and thus are to remain together. Jesus made it clear (Matthew 19:8-9) that divorce was never God's intention and was only allowed due to our own sinfulness of heart. Now, with the power of the Holy Spirit in us, we are able to seek reconciliation as a priority and not simply look for an excuse to divorce. Marriage is a life commitment, and that is why one's conduct before marriage should be taken so seriously.

The Blessings of Obedience

"And it shall come to pass, jf thou shalt hearken diligently unto the voice of the Lord thy God, to observe and to do all His comniandments which I command thee this day ... all these blessings shall come on thee, and overtake thee ... Blessed shall be the fruit of thy body ... And the Lord shall make thee plenteous ... in the fruit of thy body." - Deuteronomy 28:1-2,4,11

Virginity (obedience to God's laws as stated above) has many blessings flowing from it. The Bible declares that the fruit of the body (its reproductive process) will be blessed. This means that you can be free from unwanted pregnancies, hurry-up weddings, adoption decisions, abortion temptations, sexually transmitted diseases, hazards of birth control, loss of reputation, habitual yielding to temptation, and the forced planning of your future, simply by obeying God's laws regarding your virginity!

Virginity is such freedom! In addition to these simple blessings, we could add that the advantages of virginity include the following:

1. Guarding one's virginity saves all of your emotions and passions of sexual love for one individual. In this way, all of that stored energy of passionate giving is reserved to one individual and thus purity becomes one's foundation for marriage.

2. Virginity helps to bring security to the marriage which aids in the solid foundation for future generations.

3. The integrity of the individual believer is lifted up as a standard for others to follow demonstrating the power of Christ to preserve a life and shine in a perverse generation.

4. The testimony of the church is enhanced as a place where purity reigns and sin is overcome. We must once again restore the church with a reputation of holiness.

The Consequences of Disobedience

"... if thou wilt not hearken unto the voice of the Lord thy God, to observe to do all His commandments and His statutes which I command thee this day; that all these curses shall come upon thee, and overtake thee ... Cursed shall be the fruit of thy body... Thou shalt betroth a wife, and another man shall lie with her ... " - Deuteronomy 28:15,18,30

The consequences of deciding to lose your virginity have devastating results. God says in His word that fornication is a sin against your own body (see 1st Corinthians 6:18), and thus this could include diseases of all kinds and other malfunctions of the body in society due to widespread disobedience to this law. In addition to health hazards, we could add the potential of school dropout, low paying jobs in the future, the need for welfare support or payment (if one is a male) and a host of other huge decisions regarding potential parenting as a single parent. In addition, we could add:

1. The loss of "external virginity," where sexual passions have brought scars of rejection and callousness to the marriage bed can result. This often results in individuals having a difficult time giving themselves fully to their marriage partner.

2. The loss of "external virginity," where sexual intercourse has taken place before marriage, brings the union of another person into the marriage spiritually and thus a potential loss of security and trust. It also has the possibility of increased risk for physical disease.

3. The loss of personal integrity and character is a serious consequence today when society is trying to ignore its moral base because we hold no clear testimony of God's power to make a difference in our lives. The consequences are lifelong and one must live with them even if the scars are overcome through the love and forgiveness of the Lord and the church.

4. The loss of a testimony in the church to the world of being a wall of righteousness is a factor as well. This sets before the community around us, as well as the younger generations, a standard and example of compromise that is unfortunately hard to be missed.

What about those who have lost their virginity? Are they doomed to be second class citizens in the Kingdom of God, forever fearing the reproach of their sin before everyone else? Certainly not. There are no second class citizens in the Kingdom of God. All are treated equally before God and one another.

There is also the grace of God! Oh, what forgiveness! When understanding the seriousness of virginity, one's appreciation of the forgiveness and acceptance of both God and His church is enhanced. God forgives totally and completely, and the church is to follow His example, yet the consequences of losing one's virginity still remain.

God is able to help one overcome and be a testimony of His grace. However, He allows us to live with the consequences of sin here in this life (children born out of wedlock, habits that must be broken due to a lack of self-government when young) so that we learn that it would have been better to have obeyed Him the first time. One who has been forgiven much in this area needs to make sure their testimony is one that elevates prevention for those of the next generation rather than the repeating of the same mistakes with the offering of "cheap grace".

At the end of this chapter there is a list of Scriptures which give the heart attitude one needs in order to prevent fornication and sexual impurity. It would be wise for each individual to ponder these Scripture passages to see God's remedy for unholy affections. May God give us grace to have these implanted within our hearts!

How does one resist temptation and cultivate the appropriate heart attitudes listed on these pages? Ponder the following and build it into your life as a habitual practice before your Lord.

Overcoming Sin

"Love not the world, neither the things that are in the world. If any man love the world, the love of the Father is not in him. For all that is in the world, the lust of the flesh, and the lust of the eyes, and the pride of life, is not of the Father, but is of the world." - I John 2:15-16

"For this is the love of God, that we keep His commandments; and His commandments are not grievous. For whatsoever is born of God overcometh the world, and this is the victory that overcometh the world, even our faith." - I John 5:3-4

It all boils down to our love for God as opposed to our love for ourselves, pleasure, temporal satisfaction and sin. To overcome fornication we must exercise faith much like overcoming any other area of our life. If your heart is in love with the things of this world (lust of the flesh, lust of the eyes, or pride) then you will naturally be in love with temporal pleasures and sinful practices. It will be difficult, if not impossible, to overcome sin in this condition.

As one cultivates the proper heart attitudes (listed at the end of this chapter) through exercising faith in God, then through God's strength any type of sin can be overcome. The love of God is expressed in obedience to His commandments, which we have outlined in these first four lessons in relation to the issue of dating, sexual relationships, and true love.

We read that faith is the element which overcomes the world and sin. It is our victory! It is impossible to please God without faith (Hebrew 11:1,6.) By faith we believe in Jesus and what He did on the cross for our salvation (Romans 5:1; Ephesians 2:8.) But how do we grow in faith? We feed on the Word of God (Romans 10:17.) When the disciples asked Jesus to increase their faith, He replied:

> *"And the Lord said, if you had faith as a grain of mustard seed, you might say unto this sycamore tree, be thou plucked up by the root, and be thou planted in the sea; and it should obey you."* - Luke 17:6

What was Jesus saying? He was saying that you must start with whatever degree of faith you have even as small as a mustard seed. In other words, if you believe God can help you begin to stay pure in your thought life right now, begin there! Do not worry about tomorrow. As you exercise your faith, it will grow and magnify in the strength of the Lord. Internally, you may begin very slowly and in a small way, but externally it will magnify in a great way. This faith in the Lord is to be rooted in God's promises and commandments, or built upon His Word. Let us illustrate this in relation to overcoming the sin of the entire process of fornication from the thought to the deed.

> *"Blessed is the man that endureth temptation; for when he is tried, he shall receive the crown of life, which the Lord promised to them that love Him. Let no man say when he is tempted, I am tempted of God; for God cannot be tempted with evil, neither tempteth He any man; but every man is tempted, when he is drawn away of his own lust, and enticed. Then when lust hath conceived, it bringeth forth sin; and sin, when it is finished, bringeth forth death. Do not err, my beloved brethren. Every good and perfect gift is from above, and cometh down from the Father of Lights, with Whom is no variableness, neither shadow of turning."*
> - James 1:12-17

Heart Attitudes

Everyone of us will be tempted, to be sure. What we do with the temptation is the test. If we yield, we cannot blame God or the devil. It is our sinful lust that draws us to sin. The first step that must be overcome is when the first thought of impurity comes into our mind. It is at that moment when our faith is tested. We must reject the thought and ask God for strength to obey Him in all that we think. We must exercise faith when the first negative thought enters our mind and replace it with pure thinking from the Word of God.

We are constantly being enticed today in the area of immoral, sexual and sensual thinking through television, movies and all kinds of media and advertising. That is why it is important to control what you watch, read and feed into your mind. You cannot grow in faith while reading and feeding on sensual topics!

We can also be enticed and tempted by others, even Christians who are simply ignorant or have not controlled their own passions. That is why it is important to choose our closest friends carefully who can help edify us and strengthen our standards.

The key is to cut off sin at the roots, when it begins. If we yield, then lust is conceived, or planted in our minds and hearts. It brings forth sinful attitudes and actions which cause spiritual and even physical death if left to run its course. The consequences are devastating as we have seen. What then do we do to cut it off at the roots?

We prepare our minds ahead of time (see 1st Peter 1:13) with foresight and decide to take every thought captive to the obedience of Christ (see 2nd Corinthians 10:5). There are both positive as well as long-term planning (foresight) that must take place. This will tend to correct the lustful tendencies of our minds and hearts (taking every thought captive). The long-term precautions are outlined in detail in the next four lessons, but we need to focus right now on taking every thought captive.

1. The **first step** is to exercise faith *internally* the moment you are tempted (faith is our victory, remember?) For instance, if you find yourself constantly thinking of the opposite sex, and being drawn in a sensuous way to spend passion with your thinking, dreams or fantasies,

begin exercising faith in praying for your future mate! Ask God to keep your future mate pure, and help prepare his or her character so that it is equally prepared with yours. Ask God to help you restrain your own passions to honor God's choice for you. Pray and exercise the faith of the Lord that He will keep you and your future husband or wife. You may also pray that should God prepare you to marry one who has not been kept pure, you will extend grace and forgiveness just as God has done for you.

You will be amazed at how quickly the thoughts are taken captive because you immediately replaced lustful thoughts with Biblical faith! Faith is the *substance and evidence of things not seen* (Hebrews 13:1). You cannot see your future mate right now, but through faith you can exercise prayer on behalf of him or her, and overcome loneliness, sensual temptation and lustful thinking. In fact, the heart of exercising faith is the faithfulness of God and this character trait being worked in your own life. Be faithful to God and He will keep you faithful in purity and preserve you for your future mate!

2. The **second step** is to exercise faith *externally* in order to guard your own feelings and emotions. Internal faith deals with your thoughts, but external faith deals with your actions. In Ist John 5:18 The Lord says *"we know that whatsoever is born of God sinneth not; but he that is begotten of God keepeth* (or guards) *himself, and that wicked one toucheth him not."* Just as you wrestle with exercising faith internally, take action externally to prevent temptation, so you are protected even if you fall for tempting thoughts and do not immediately send them fleeing from you.

This can be done by talking to your father and/or mother and asking them to help you build fences to help guard your emotions. This is part of "keeping yourself pure" as the Bible commands. None of us can do this alone in isolation without covenant relationships. Leave no place for the devil in your mind (see Ephesians 4:27.)

What is our conclusion?

We must embrace a vision of virginity for our marriages. We must recognize clearly the blessings of obedience and the consequences of disobedience.

We must ponder this - for this is the key to preventing havoc in life later on. Take time to pray and purpose in your heart that you will not be defiled in any way, from the thoughts to the deed.

We must *flee fornication*!

We must separate ourselves as far from the process as possible. This will require embracing the right heart attitudes that overcome fornication, and then letting our actions follow. Remember, all sin, including fornication, begins in the heart.

Faith is the Victory!

Finally we must *exercise faith*!

The exercise of faith in your life will change your heart, cultivate pure desires, prevent sin, and overcome temptation. As we exercise even the smallest aspect of faith (belief in God's Word and His will,) we will grow and gain more control over sin and all of its consequences. This involves preventing thoughts from becoming patterns in your mind, as well as guarding your actions with help from others.

Is this all possible? Can a teenage generation buck the tide and keep itself pure for the purpose of fulfilling the highest call of God in their lives? Is it possible to live your life above the traps of sin, selfishness, and the devil? The Bible verses below offer us a promise that, with God's help, we can live above sin and its bondage:

> *"Wherewithal shall a young man cleanse his way? by taking heed thereto according to thy word. With my whole heart have I sought thee; 0 let me not wander from thy commandments. Thy word have I hid in mine heart, that I might not sin against thee."*
> - Psalm 119:9-11

> *"Whosoever abideth in him sinneth not... Whosoever is born of God doth not commit sin; for his seed remaineth in him; and he cannot sin, because he is born of God." * - I John 3:6a, 9

Biblical Chart of Heart Attitudes Toward Sexual Purity

Scripture Verse on Heart Attitudes	Pure Heart Attitudes	Sinful Heart Attitudes
"... that they abstain from pollution of idols, and from fornication..." (Acts 15:20)	Abstinence from sinful thoughts	Indulgence in sinful thoughts
"... God gave them over to a reprobate mind... being filled with all... fornication... (Romans 1:28-29)	Pleasure in God and His purposes	Pleasure in sin and its wickedness
"I wrote you in an epistle not to company with fornicators, yet not altogether with the fornicators of this world." (1st Corinthians 5:9-10)	Caution with the company one keeps so one is pure enough to reach out to others	Bad company corrupts good morals, especially with believing fornicators
"Be not deceived... fornicators... shall not inherit the kingdom of God" (1st Corinthians 6:9)	Compassion for the lost and where fornication leads	Condemnation of the lost and saved who are careless
"Now the body is for the Lord and the Lord is for the body." (1st Corinthians 6:18)	Purity in body given to the Lord	Impurity in body given to sin
"Flee fornication." (1st Corinthians 6:18)	Separation from a sinful environment	Live dangerously in sinful environments
"Every sin that a man doeth is without the body, but he	Bringing blessings upon your own	Bringing judgment upon

that commiteth fornication sinneth against his own body." (1st Corinthians 6:18)	body as a vessel for the Lord's use	your body with hindered use in the Lord's work
"It is good for a man not to touch a woman." (1st Corinthians 7:1)	<u>Respecting</u> the opposite sex - no defrauding	<u>Arousing</u> and defrauding the opposite sex
"...neither let us commit fornication... let him that thinketh he standeth take heed lest he fall." (1st Corinthians 10:8, 11)	<u>Humility</u> before the Lord, living in fear of Him	<u>Pride</u> in yourself and having no fear of God before you
"and that I shall bewail many which have sinned already, and have not repented of the uncleaness and fornication and lasciviousness which they have committed." (2nd Corinthians 12:21)	<u>A Soft Conscience</u> in repentance before the Lord	<u>A Seared Conscience</u> with no repentance before the Lord
"Now the works of the flesh are these; adultery, fornication, uncleaness, lasciviousness." (Galatians 5:19)	<u>Spiritual thinking</u> is cultivated	<u>Carnal thinking</u> is cultivated
"But fornication and all uncleaness or covetousness.. neither filthiness, nor foolish talking... but rather giving of thanks." (Ephesians 5:3-4)	<u>Grateful</u> heart leads to upholding holy standards	<u>Ungrateful</u> heart leads to letting down standards

"Mortify therefore your members... fornication, uncleanness, inordinate affection, evil concupiscence" (Colossians 3:5)	<u>Crucifying</u> sinful thoughts is the way of the cross	<u>Indulging</u> sinful thoughts is the way of self
"That no man go beyond and defraud his brother in any manner.. for God hath not called us unto uncleanness but unto holiness." (1st Thessalonians 4:4-9)	<u>Protecting</u> one another is guarding the weaknesses of others in order to preserve holiness	<u>Defrauding</u> one another is taking advantage of their weakness in sexual passion

It is for this reason that we now focus our attention in the remainder of this course on God's replacement for the dating process. If dating does not work, what does?

How can one begin to prepare as a teenager for marriage?

How can one build proper fences in his life to avoid the common pitfalls of individuals who later wish they had done so?

These and more questions will be answered as we continue our study together of God's standards for our heart attitudes and our actions toward the opposite sex.

Lesson Five

TEAM MINISTRY:
GOD'S ALTERNATIVE TO DATING

What is Team Ministry? A team consists of two or more individuals working together to achieve a common goal or purpose. Noah Webster defines the Saxon root of the word to mean "offspring, progeny, or race of descendants". In Webster's day (early 1800's), a team meant a group of animals yoked or harnessed together to pull a coach or vehicle of some kind. There were no athletic teams or other more modern illustrations that we would think of today. The closest analogy to today might have been an army that would work together to achieve the goal of liberty. However, due to the origin of the word, when involving people, it was most often used to describe a long line of descendants such as a race of people, thus including several generations.

The most basic team is the marriage unit. It is the foundation for generations of descendants. It is out of this team that God chose to spread life, liberty and the protection of property in the earth. One of the reasons for the high rate of divorce in America and the world is the fact that individuals have no habit of working together in teams prior to marriage. They live for themselves, their own pleasure, and no one is to interfere with this self-serving attitude.

Obviously, when married, individuals continue what they began while young. They do not know how to work for the common good of all, deny selfish desires for the sake of others or realize the satisfaction of accomplishing something together that could not be accomplished apart. Habits are hard to break, even with the greatest of intentions. You see, this is at the heart of why the dating pattern must be replaced. We need much better preparation for team work.

When God created mankind, He did so as a picture of His Image. God is a team. The Father, Son and Holy Spirit work together constantly on our behalf. The whole redemption story is the story of a team willing to sacrifice. The Father willingly sacrificed His Son, the Son sacrificed His life, and the Holy Spirit took on the challenge of uniting believers into teamwork so that they could accomplish something in unity. The "Godhead" is a team!

The family is to operate in His Image. Father, mother and children are to work together, sacrificing what is necessary for the goal of fulfilling God's call in the earth. Thus, we must see that team ministry and practice in working together as a team are critical to preparing for marriage and family life later on.

The first team you need to focus on is what we might call our "internal team," our family. We call it internal because much of what you do there is not readily visible to others. However, the habits you build at home, working with your family as a team, will become visible when you endeavor to do the same in some "external team." External teams are usually extended at school or church. This is where we learn to work with those outside our family for common goals or purposes. What we say in this lesson will always be held in this context - first to be applied in the internal team of your own family, and then extended to team work in the school or church. Whether this includes athletic teams or a choir, the same principles apply.

Key Ingredients in Team Ministry

In the following Scripture passage we have several key elements listed about the advantages of team work. We could call them key ingredients in team ministry. We will briefly take a look at these five essential ingredients, and then expand them for the remainder of this lesson.

> *"Then I returned, and I saw vanity under the sun. There is one alone, and there is not a second; yea, he hath neither child not brother; yet is there no end of all his labor; neither is his eye satisfied with riches; neither saith he, for whom do I labor, and bereave my soul of good? This is also vanity, yea, it is a sore travail. Two are better than one because they have a*

good reward for their labor. For if they fall, the one will lift up his fellow; but woe to him that is alone when he falleth; for he hath not another to help him up. Again, if two lie together, then they have heat but how can one be warm alone? And if one prevail against him, two shall withstand him; and a threefold cord is not quickly broken." - Ecclesiastes 4:7-12

It is vanity to endeavor to accomplish all that God has called you to do alone. As the verses state above, there will not be as great a reward when you labor alone. Let us look at five key ingredients of team ministry noted in these verses.

1. *"There is one alone, there is not a second.. he hath neither child nor brother."* In other words, a team **joins the generations**. When neither a child or brother will help you, you do not even have the most basic team - a family. Team work is an extension of the family unit and extends the kind of character learned at home to bless others. Your relationships at home prepare you for team ministry. A team provides a balance of multi-generations - all ages working together.

2. *"Neither saith he, for whom do I labor, and bereave my soul of good?"* A team must have a **purpose** to serve or minister in some way. Otherwise, there is no reason to continue on and sacrifice what is necessary for the good of all. When vision is diminished, and purposes unclear, people are not as willing to see the need of working together. When an individual is alone, he quickly loses heart; and sacrifice is a drudgery. A team embraces a goal beyond itself, and this provides a necessary ingredient for its success.

3. *"Two are better than one; because they have a good reward for their labor."* Team ministry provides **greater success** than we could ever have alone. That is what a "good reward" is all about. There is just nothing like the satisfaction of accomplishing something after working hard together.

4. *"For if they fall, the one will lift up his fellow; but woe to him that is alone when he falleth; for he hath not another to help him up."* Team ministry is preparation in building **friendships**. It is the true basis for fellowship. Working together to fulfill a goal beyond what you could do yourself opens you up to knowing others. The focus is not on each other, but on the goal. However, the safest context for friendship is working side by side to see something accomplished.

5. *"And if one prevail against him, two shall withstand him; and a threefold cord is not quickly broken"*. Another key ingredient in team work is **covenantal protection**. We are stronger together than we are apart. We might be defeated if working alone, but together we cannot be easily defeated. A threefold "cord" refers to a covenant. We agree to protect each other from all kinds of danger as we work together.

Joining the Generations

"...you younger, submit yourselves unto the elder. Yea; all of you be subject one to another, and be clothed with humility, for God resisteth the proud, and giveth grace to the humble." - I Peter 5:5

Honor

There are two vital points for us to consider here. First of all, it is always in God's order for the "younger" to have a natural **honor** and submission to those who are older. This involves respect, obedience (especially when authority is involved) and a general looking to elders for direction and advice. It also includes the fact that those who are older should be working with those that are younger. There is an aspect here of joining the generations that begins in the family and is extended out to other spheres of ministry and influence.

Team ministry provides a context where one can learn submission to authority (parents and adults,) yet have a vital part in making the team work and fulfill its goals. This balance is critical to learn. The Bible tells us to honor our parents, no matter how old we are. This

70

means that the respect due them will last long after we have left home and established our own homes. Thus, it is important to cultivate now the right attitude to those who are older than you are. For example, we could list the following key attitudes that we need to embrace in order to practice this first aspect of **honor** in joining the generations:

1. A *submissive attitude* at all times should be cultivated toward those older than ourselves. They have lived longer. A special place of honor is kept for our parents. We should honor their presence on any team at any time. We should not find ourselves being too quick to criticize those that are older - but willing to submissively respect all opinions and advice. This is primarily an attitude, regardless of whether you personally agree or disagree with the older individual, adult in authority, or your own parents.

2. *Obedience* should be given to instructions received from those in authority over you. There are times for discussion and counsel in a team - but not when asked to do things. If we are told to do something, we obey cheerfully. The time to discuss it may be later. However, we owe honor and respect to those in authority at all times and this will help prepare us for employment and our own positions of authority in the future. Only those who have learned to obey can become good leaders who can give sound and wise instruction.

3. Our attitudes toward those younger than we are should also be *encouraging* and respectful. Those who are younger are drawn to respect us when we care and go out of our way to include them in any way we can. We are not interested in forming "cliques" and small groups which ostracize others, and a team is an excellent place where such lessons can be learned well. If we want our younger brothers and sisters, as well as younger students to respect us, and even obey us if we are placed in authority over them, then their respect is needed.

Humility

A second key aspect spoken of in this verse that illustrates what joining the generations really means is **humility**. We are told that we are to be subject one to another and be clothed with **humility**. Some key attitudes we can embrace in this area are the following:

1. We are all to *mutually respect one another*, regardless of age, in relation to any function of team ministry. Our function may require our giving account in an area, and it may mean that there are those working with us who are older, but submitted in attitude unto us, helping us learn to take the lead. This is a beautiful balance. We must always be willing to respect one another for the greater purpose of the team.

2. One of the benefits of joining the generations in team ministry is the *weeding out of pride*. If youth begin to think they can do things without adults, pride sets in and usually results in more rules and the need for more authority on the part of adults. On the other hand, if adults feel that youth have no valuable input on a team, then disappointment will be added to the disrespect shown by youth. The mutual submission (pointed out in the above paragraph) is one of the greatest blessings one could ever experience on a team.

3. Now let us talk about the quality of *humility*. As we clothe ourselves with humility - realizing that only Jesus deserves the greatest reward - we have a tremendous chance of defeating the enemy and bringing God's purposes into being. God resists the proud, but gives grace unto the humble. His presence and acceptance will be the reward of humbling ourselves before one another. This means an honesty as well as an integrity of respect and submission.

In what way can joining the generations as a part of team ministry be helpful in preparation for marriage as a replacement for the dating process?

The practice of joining the generations is a practice in *family relationships*. The practicing of submission and leadership (whether or not you agree with the person) prepares you for the marriage relationship. Honoring your parents prepares you for training your children to honor you. Learning to express differences and give advice in a spirit of humility prepares you for harmony in your home later in life. Finally, learning to sacrifice and work with those of a younger age prepares you for working in harmony with your own children rather than selfishly pursuing your own goals at their expense.

Purpose

"...upon this rock I will build my church; and the gates of hell shall not prevail against it. And I will give unto thee the keys of the kingdom of heaven; and whatsoever thou shalt bind on earth shall be bound in heaven; and whatsoever thou shalt loose on earth shall be loosed in heaven." - Matthew 16:18-19

"Again I say unto you, that if two of you shall agree on earth as touching any thing that they shall ask, it shall be done for them of my Father which is in heaven. For where two or three are gathered together in my name, there am I in the midst of them." - Matthew 18:19-20

Purpose is a key concept in team ministry. We do not meet, work or be together just to relate or get to know one another. This is the great mistake of the youth group or any group whose goal is merely social. The distractions of social goals will slowly deceive us into thinking that meeting my relational needs will result in spiritual fulfillment. It is only in reaching for our spiritual destiny that we will find our social needs met. We join together as adults and youth, knowing that together we can kick in the gates of hell!

If you haven't guessed it by now, the type of team ministry we are talking about is simply the reality of living in church life in a practical way that involves youth of all ages. A team must have a purpose beyond itself if it is to be successful.

The universal church spoken of by Jesus is called to destroy the gates of hell, and those gates will not be able to withstand the church. In the second passage Jesus speaks of the local church, or a local team, and its purpose is to restore relationships. The order is important. As we pursue God's call and vision for team ministry, relationships will be restored and maintained. Only in the context of team vision and purpose can we maintain the kind of relationships spoken of earlier. Consider some of the following attitudes we must embrace:

1. Fulfilling God's *vision* through ministry is exciting and full of adventure. Learning to pray, fast, teach, and preach the Word of God together builds a solid foundation for the future church. We as adults must run with youth at the same speed before giving them the baton. We need to embrace a vision as youth that we can practice living in the true church - built on relationships - before we have to have the responsibilities of authority! That is a blessing you will always cherish the rest of your life.

2. It is in *intense ministry* with great purpose that God intends for us to discern our future mate. God's call is most important. As we work side by side, with another individual in ministry, his or her character, ability to be consistent under pressure, and true motives are discerned. It is this type of calling that should draw us to another in Christ. After all, the primary purpose of getting married is to fulfill your part in the expansion of the Kingdom together with another in a greater way than you could individually and independently. This helps one to avoid the traps of deception and blindness that can occur when courtship begins.

How can intense ministry help prepare us for marriage?

The environment of intense ministry and vision extending to multi-generations is the best context in which to **discern one's future mate**. God's call upon each life must be equally yoked. Often we think

74

that if another individual is a Christian, and a nice one, then certainly marriage could be Biblical. "Equally yoked" means far more than this. The most important aspect of getting married is to discern God's call and the intensity of it in the other individual. Marriages that do not begin in ministry usually do not continue in ministry. It is much harder to produce ministry later on, and it also wastes valuable years. Most of the adult generation today had to take the time for God to restore their callings and ministry whereas the next generation can have a head start! Let's go for the gold!

Increasing Our Success

"We then that are strong ought to bear the infirmities of the weak, and not to please ourselves. Let every one of us please his neighbor for his good to edification... that we through patience and comfort of the scriptures might have hope. Now the God of patience and consolation grant you to be like-minded one toward another according to Christ Jesus; that you may with one mind and one mouth glorify God, even the Fattier of our Lord Jesus Christ." - Romans 15:1-6

The success we can experience as a team is far more than we could achieve as individuals. That is one of the main purposes of having a team. In a team, we learn to look for one anther's success more than our own. We are willing to share our strengths where others are weak. We understand that working together in unity produces a greater effect in glorifying God in both power and wisdom. Some key attitudes we can embrace that will help our success are the following:

1. Every one of us is talented and has *strengths*. We also have *weaknesses*. No one is perfect. It is this combination, in all ages, that makes a team so dynamic. Embracing this attitude will help us work together and see all of our gifts released to bless others. We must embrace the attitude that every individual has value equally with everyone, but not everyone has the same strengths or weaknesses.

2. Our ability to *lovingly work with each other* will improve each one of our weaknesses and help us become stronger. We can actually begin to glory (or give God thanks) for our weaknesses - knowing that as we are willing to admit them, the power of Christ can meet us at this point of humility. Correction, evaluation, and setting goals for improvement will help us all to become stronger individually.

3. *Overcoming discouragement* is another asset of team ministry. When one is down, another is up. When one is discouraged, another is encouraged. As we learn to encourage one another and provoke one another to love and good works, we will begin to see that God designed us to work together in harmony so that together we could manifest a greater degree of consistency for the world to see. The Bible declares that our unity and harmony will be the greatest testimony to the world that Jesus Christ indeed is real.

How can this working together with our strengths and weaknesses better replace the dating pattern?

By learning to release our gifts and improve our weaknesses, we prepare for **growth** in our future marriage. Successful marriages are built upon a solid estimation of each partner and his weaknesses or gifts. Individuals who go into marriage with fantasy-land dreams of perfection and no real experience learning from others can be married for years without affecting growth or change in either partner. Marriage partners often have no vision of the strengths in the other, and thus domination by husband or wife is the result.

Building Friendships

"That no man go beyond and defraud his brother in any matter... for ye yourselves are taught of God to love one another." - I Thessalonians 4:6,9

True friendships are another blessing of team ministry. True friends are hard to come by today - but they are a necessary ingredient for one to prepare for marriage. Next to one's spiritual destiny and calling, learning to build solid friendships is the most important aspect of preparing for the marriage relationship.

First comes the act of leaving one's old life for a new one (spiritual calling and destiny,) and then comes the act of cleaving to your wife or husband. This act of cleaving is another way of saying that one has formed a covenant of friendship. It involves the soul, and its nature is social. Although the next lesson deals in detail with building true friends, let us state some of the key attitudes that need to be embraced as a replacement for the dating process:

1. Learning to *build many friendships* is a positive way of extending the family into the church. Although all of us should be friendly with those outside the church, true deep friends are those you can trust spiritually, socially, and even physically. Building true friends can take place very easily within team ministry. That is because the focus is on several individuals rather than on pairing up with one individual. Building the kinds of bridges necessary for true friendship is essential in preparation for marriage.

2. The expression of *natural affection* is another attitude that can be built within true friendship. Natural affection is simply the common care and concern for one another that is expressed in some external way. From a slap on the back to an embrace out of pure love and not out of a sensual motive (defrauding) builds trust and acceptance. Although most natural affection occurs with those of the same sex (and is the safest and wisest policy,) it is possible that a team could grow so close as to allow natural affection between both guys and girls without sensual motives or pairing up.

How does this prepare one for a godly and Biblical marriage?

Next to one's destiny and calling, **true friendship and communication** is the most necessary ingredient for a healthy marriage. Many marriages involve individuals existing together with little or no communication. If the marriage began in an atmosphere emphasizing merely sensual self-gratification, then the foundation laid is not strong enough to deal with everyday living. The amount of time spent in meaningful communication once married far outweighs that spent in the physical realm. Thus, a practical foundation to lay in your life is that of communication and friendship. We need a new generation willing to restore true friendship as a basis for the marriage relationship. This can occur most naturally through team ministry.

Covenantal Protection

"Be sober, be vigilant; because your adversary the devil, as a roaring lion, walketh about, seeking whom he may devour; whom resist steadfast in the faith, knowing that the same afflictions are accomplished in your brethren that are in the world." - I Peter 5:8-9

It takes only common sense to perceive that our enemy is out to destroy the home. He recognizes that the best way to destroy the home is not only to attack marriages and family relationships, but destroy the foundation of the home before it gets started. Thus, the symptoms of those who simply live together with no real commitment: fornication and sensual lifestyles are a large part of his strategy.

The Bible declares above that the devil is like a roaring lion, desiring to devour individuals. However, he *can never devour a true Biblical team!* We will need to fight his attacks with more than individual desires and isolated ministries - we need a team.

We saw earlier that a team has an advantage in war - two or more can defend better than one. So it is with team ministry. One great advantage is to have others who will fight for you - protect you when you are not looking or alert, so you are not deceived and the enemy can get no advantage over you. Consider some of the following attitudes to embrace in this area:

1. Team ministry allows us to openly and honestly *declare our intentions* as a natural family, church, school, or any group of youth and adults. Before we are in temptation, one great foresight is to set the fences and boundaries clearly in writing. In this way we can all agree, when not under great temptation and duress, to protect one another from anything that should arise that would draw us in the wrong direction. This helps to prevent problems ahead of time by utilizing a covenant agreement. An example of this covenant will be given in lesson six of this book.

2. Another key attitude, in addition to prevention, is to watch over each other, being our *brother's and sister's keeper*. When attitudes and actions become loose, we can help each other become what we have stated and rise to the occasion. We can protect each other from outside influences and attitudes that we find ourselves in from time to time, even in ministry. The attitude of preventing even the appearance of evil is hardly popular today, and thus we need to be on guard. From women desiring to be prayed for specifically by men, or teenage boys feeling a call to evangelize good looking teenage girls, we have much deception clothed in religious language that tends to weaken our standards and testimony. A team dedicated to protecting one another goes a long way toward solving these problems.

How does this covenant of protection relate to our preparation of a Godly lifestyle for marriage?

Marriage is a **covenant**. It is a covenant of protection one for the other. It is also a covenant of protection and responsibility toward children. It also teaches us how to live practically in a situation where we care for one another, and thus will relate to the way we care for our spouse, children and others in the future church to which God has called us to minister.

Learning to **guard each other's purity** through the means of a stated covenant is the foundation for what a family and church is all about. We need to raise the standard for the next generation in relation to holiness and purity in the church of Jesus Christ!

Team Ministry Contrasted with the Dating Pattern

In summary, the ingredient of *joining the generations* helps prepare us in cultivating the honor and humility so needed in our future family relationships. The ingredient of *purpose and ministry* prepares us to properly discern our future mate through the eyes of their calling in God. The *increased success* we experience in complementing our strengths and weaknesses prepares us for growth in the marriage relationship. This will also help us avoid the pitfalls and mistakes of past generations. The ingredient of *building friendships* helps prepare us for true communication in marriage - probably the greatest weakness in marriages today. Finally, *covenantal protection* cultivated in team ministry helps to prepare us for guarding our marriage and its purity before God, defeating the enemy's schemes for the destruction of the family.

Let us now contrast team ministry with the dating pattern:

Team Ministry	**The Dating Pattern**
1. Focus one's attention on <u>ministry</u> as a team.	1. Focus one's attention on <u>pairing up</u> as a couple.
2. Work at <u>giving</u> through the joining of generations at home, church and school to build relationships.	2. Work at <u>getting</u> your partner's attention through flirting for the sake of physical pleasure.
3. Learning to <u>complement</u> strengths and weaknesses so that the team is stronger and weaknesses are overcome.	3. Coming together as a result of gaining one another's attention through general likes and <u>compatibility</u> physically.

4. Learning to <u>discern</u> one's future mate through intensity of ministry and the call of God.

4. Getting <u>emotionally</u> <u>involved</u> to fulfill each other's desire for company - physically or socially.

5. Learning to build <u>many friends</u> through loyalty, honesty and integrity toward all.

5. Becoming <u>attached</u> to each other affectionately, so that as a couple you <u>exclude</u> other friends.

6. <u>Covenanting</u> to protect one another's purity and value so that the enemy finds no door of rejection to destroy the team.

6. <u>Defrauding</u> one another by stealing one another's affection, breaking up, pairing up again, and forming a pattern of rejection.

Ponder the above, and really ask yourself a question:

Which will better prepare you for a wholesome life?
Which has greater risks?
Which will aid you in fulfilling God's call upon your life?
Which will lay a greater foundation for your marriage?

In answering these questions, you will need to pray, seek the Lord, and come to a conclusion (and conviction) based upon the evidence Biblically, not simply because your parents, or any other adult wants you to. If these convictions exist, then you are prepared to really put your intentions into action.

That is what the next lesson is all about - cultivating true friends in an atmosphere of team ministry.

Lesson Six

CULTIVATING TRUE FRIENDSHIPS

Understanding Biblical Love

"So when they had dined, Jesus said to Simon Peter, Simon, son of Jonas, do you love Me more than these? He said unto him, Yea, Lord, You know that I love You. He said unto him, Feed My lambs. He said to him again the second time, Simon, son of Jonas, do you love Me? He said unto him, Yea, Lord; You know that I love You. He said unto him, Feed My sheep. He said unto him the third time, Simon, son of Jonas, do you love Me? Peter was grieved because He said unto him the third time, Do you love Me? And he said unto Him, Lord, You know all things; You know that I love You. Jesus said unto him, Feed my sheep." - John 21:15-17

On the surface, that conversation seems a bit hard on Peter. After all, if you were asked the same question three times, you would be a little annoyed as well! However, when we look beneath the King James translation, we find that there are two Greek words used for love in the passage. They are very distinct, and both have distinct purposes as used by the Lord. They are at two different levels of spirituality. In essence, the Lord Jesus was endeavoring to have Peter understand that his love for Him was not at the level that it should be.

The first word, most commonly understood to mean Divine love, or God's love, is the Greek word *agape*. This word was not even used until the New Testament came into being. There was no parallel for it in the Greek culture either. Thus, much of its cultural meaning remains a mystery in the study of words. However, since it is so characteristic in the New Testament, it has significant meaning to us. It denotes a totally unselfish giving, and is used for God giving us His Son, as well as what our love should be like toward God. There is no thought of return in agape. As one authority put it, it expresses "the essential nature of God."[5] It is used of our love to God and one another.

It is this word that Jesus uses when confronting Peter, *"do you love me more than these?,"* and then again *"do you love me?"* In the third question that Jesus asks, He uses a different word, condescending to the same one used by Peter each time in his answer. This second word, translated love again in the King James but meaning something entirely different in the Greek, is *phileo*. It is never used in the Bible as a command to love God. It is a friendship love. It is used for tender affection and brother-sister type love. It is the natural love for our fellow man, but lacks the holy and awesome reverence attached to *agape* which is used for our love of God.

What is the point in this distinction? Jesus first asks Peter if He loves Him with *agape*. Since Peter answers that he does love Him with *phileo* or natural affection, Jesus continues to ask the question, making the clear distinction in Greek that we might not notice in the English translation. Finally, he uses Peter's word *phileo* the third time. Jesus was defining the only type of love relationship that is designed for walking with God, and out from which we must love each other. It is a supernatural love that is the basis for a true relationship with God rather than a casual friendship relationship. This is where it all begins. *If we love God, we will keep His commandments.*

Notice that in all three questions, Jesus instructs Peter that a result of his love for Him would be to feed or shepherd others. Giving is always the primary characteristic of Christian love. Giving in order to get is *phileo*, but giving regardless of what is returned is *agape*. The first is natural, the second is supernatural. We probably all began understanding our love for Jesus in terms of merely being our friend. However, this word is used negatively and positively in the Bible, depending upon whether *agape* characteristics are involved. For example, it is possible to love life and others from a purely selfish motive, which is not of God.

---

[5] Vine, W.E., *An Expository Dictionary of New Testament Words* (Old Tappan, NJ, Fleming H. Revell, 1940), page 74.

What is our point here? Simply this: God desires for us to cultivate His love, first in our relationship with Him, and then with each other. The natural love of a brother and sister, *phileo*, is nurtured in a secure home where affection and loyalty come with familiarity. However, in natural love there is often the idea that we are owed some reward for our giving - it is giving and getting in reciprocal fashion.

The primary characteristic of *agape* will be to give endlessly, caring for each other and doing only that which will help one another come closer to the Lord, regardless of whether it is returned in like manner. This is only possible if God's love is flowing through us, because it does not originate in our own nature, it originates in God's nature. We must learn to love in His love, give in His love, and serve in His love. Our own natural love, strength, and desire will run dry very quickly since it is usually compared with how much people are going out of their way for us.

If you attempt to love God with *phileo*, you will often be disappointed because your affections for God will be determined by how well you think God has taken care of you (by your own definition). Also, if you endeavor to love others out of our own love, from a human viewpoint, it can turn sour due to the frailty of your own sinful nature. We can begin to use people for our own advantage, even our friends! We use friendships to accomplish what we desire, and if we attempt to love God with *phileo* we attempt to use our relationship with God to achieve our own desires through manipulation! We can even make friends with God and others with ulterior motives in mind like getting to know someone because they know someone else or getting to know God so you can get a good experience. This is a humanistic version of *phileo*.

Only from the context of *agape* can we truly love one another and build friendships that will be positive and edifying. This was Jesus' message to Peter. Only when we love God with *agape* (His love,) can we then properly minister to others.

It is important for each and every one of us to know that God has given us His love (*agape*) at the moment of salvation (Romans 5:5-8). However, we need to rest in it, and let it be released by faith unto God and one another. Jesus prayed that the same love (*agape*) that His

Father had loved Him with would be manifested through us (John 17:26). This is so important. If we do not start where God starts, we cannot end where God ends.

Each of us needs to go back to God, to the Well of life within us, and ask Him for a Divine love for Him and one another. Only when we do this can we begin to see true friendship occur with each other. This begins with asking God to reveal His love to us. His love is unending, even when we do not deserve it, and even when we do not return it to Him. Then, ask Him to allow that to be given out from us to one another. It is from this context that we will be able to build true bridges of friendship with each other.

Another word used in Greek culture for love is the word *eros*. Although it does not occur readily in the New Testament, words similar to it do occur. It means sexual love. It is the love between a man and his wife that is expressed in a physical way. Once again, this love has its place, but can be abused, as we have seen, when in the context of getting pleasure outside of the boundaries and laws that God has given us for our protection. Humanistically speaking, sexual pleasure becomes the goal when *eros* is pursued outside of God's purposes. You end up seeking pleasure rather than the other person's best interest and that is why it can cause terrible consequences. People murder for it, rape for it, and lust after it. This is not true *eros* expressed out of *agape*, but rather an animalistic eros, reducing us to animal desires as illustrated in the expanded definitions of related words in Lesson Four.

Agape love is primarily spiritual, and can only be expressed by God Himself. When Christ lives in our heart by faith due to conversion, this love can be expressed by faith in our love for God and others. *Phileo* relates to the soul for it is a social friendship kind of love. When governed by *agape*, its potential abuse can be curbed, and we can experience a brother-sister type of love as a team, expressing affection that is not seductive. *Eros* relates to the body, and is reserved for the expression of love between one man and one woman in marriage.

Eros expressed out of an *agape* motive of unselfish love is illustrated by C.S. Lewis in a man's love for his wife:

85

"Now Eros makes a man really want, not a woman, but one particular woman. In some mysterious but quiet indisputable fashion the lover desires the Beloved herself, not the pleasure she can give."[6]

In other words, true sexual love out of *agape* seeks the individual and not merely the pleasure they can receive. It is not possible for a young man to steal the passion and virginity away from a young girl when he moves in *agape love*. This only occurs when *eros* is in control through the guise of *phileo*. When under the control of God's love, one would seek what is best for the other individual according to the will of God, not the will of selfish pleasure.

Just as it is a dangerous trend for our love for God to be illustrated through *phileo* alone, so it is every more dangerous for our love for God to be illustrated through *eros*. The downward spiral of sensual pleasure and selfishness has taken us to expressing our love for God now in *eros* terms. Thus, we speak of having "passion for God" as if it was passion for sexual pleasure, or "looking into God's eyes" as if we are preparing to kiss our lover, and now God is even "madly in love with us," as if we are seeking sexual pleasure in our relationship with Him!

One indication of danger is when our love from God or for God is expressed without the fear (reverence and respect) for God. It is the fear of God that is the beginning (or most important part) of knowledge.[7] It is this element, coupled with the submissive elements of both social and physical love that is in balance in the Song of Solomon, the book in the Bible that uses the marriage relationship of love at all levels with our love for God Himself.

You see, one can understand why we should treat one another properly, refraining from dating relationships, and keeping ourselves pure, so that we have time to learn how to fear God, keep His commandments, and express all levels of love out from *agape*. The main ingredient is God's love. This is the most important part, for it is a

---

[6] Lewis, C.S., *The Four Loves* (Harcourt, Brace and Jovanovich, Boston, MA, 1960), page 75.

[7] see Proverbs 1:7; 9:10; 14:26-27; 15:16, 33

deep respect and reverence for His nature. It can keep us from consequences like venereal disease, AIDS, and emotional and physical scars of rejection. Though we understand the consequences of disobeying the Lord's commandments, none of these things alone will keep us in the hour of temptation. Only *agape*, given from God, and released by yielding our will and surrendering to His strength, will be able to keep us in every situation. For only then will we be interested in others more than ourselves.

Consider a quick overview of *agape love* from 1st Corinthians 13:4-8a (New American Standard translation). As we ponder its Divine characteristics, we need to ask God to allow it to flow forth like a river to one another, baptizing us all in the love of The Lord:

"Love is patient" (endures through any hardship)

"Love is kind" (respects all people and is polite)

"Love is not jealous" (does not compete for attention)

"Love does not brag" (is not proud)

"Love is not arrogant" (does not bring attention to itself)

"Love does not act unbecomingly" (is not rude)

"Love does not seek its own" (does not put self first)

"Love is not provoked" (is not irritated with another's failure)

"Love does not take into account a wrong suffered" (does not
     hold grudges)

"Love does not rejoice in unrighteousness" (does not enjoy evil)

"Love rejoices with the truth" (loves what is Godly and right)

"Love bears all things" (puts up with others in toleration)

"Love believes all things" (is always positive and full of faith)

"Love hopes all things" (is always filled with vision)

"Love endures all things" (is consistent in all situations)

"Love never fails" (will always be the same)

Let us agree to cultivate and release the kind of love God gave us at Calvary! He gave with no expectation of return, though He knew that His love would draw you to Him. He gave and would still give even if you turned your back on Him. Though His justice gives boundary and meaning to His love, *agape* continues to give because *God is love.*

The beautiful thing about it is that He has given us this love to share with others. Let us agree to release this first; and then the friendships, natural affection, and sexual love will find its proper place of expression under the guidance of *agape* which fulfills God's Law.

Biblical Friendship

Everyone loves to have friends. However, we often do not define the word as clearly as we ought to. What ideas should we have in mind about the kind of friends we seek? What do our close friends reveal about our attitudes and true motives? For these answers and others, let us define friendship:

> *"One who is attached to another by affection; one who entertains for another sentiments of esteem, respect and affection, which lead him to desire his company, and to seek to promote his happiness and prosperity"* - Webster's 1828 Dictionary

The Biblical word *phileo* has the implication of "*close associate,*" or "*neighbor,*" and is used in the context or picture of those who pasture in the same area or field. It is companionship.[8] In other words, friends work together for the same goal or purpose. In choosing friends, the Bible warns:

> *"Do not be deceived: bad company corrupts good morals."* - I Corinthians 15:33

In 1823, Noah Webster wrote to letter to a young person beginning his college education. It could be taken as a short commentary on the above verse of Scripture. In dealing with forming friends, he said the following:

> *"In forming your connections in society, be careful to select for your companions, young men of good*

---

[8] See *Strong's Concordance*, Baker Book House, 1989, word #5384.

> *breeding, and of virtuous principles and habits. The company of the profligate and irreligious is to be shunned as poison. You cannot always avoid some intercourse with men of dissolute lives; but you can always select, for your intimate associates, men of good principles and unimpeachable character. Never maintain a familiar intercourse with the profane, the lewd, the intemperate, the gamester, or the scoffer at religion. Towards men of such character, the common civilities of life are to be observed - beyond these, nothing is required of men who reverence the divine precepts, and who desire, to 'keep themselves unspotted from the world.'"[9]*

In summary, we could say that the definition of friendship involves some of the following key concepts:

1. We choose the friends that demonstrate what we hold to be most valuable in life. We esteem the qualities most evident in our friends. We choose friends that we wish to be like. In other words, our close friends are external illustrations of our heart desires.

2. Our friends are companions to help us fulfill common goals. A friend will work with you to achieve Godly goals, not hinder you.

3. Our own moral standards can be corrupted when choosing those who demonstrate different values than our own; thus great discernment is essential in choosing friends wisely.

4. Being friendly is different from true friendship. We should be friendly to all, but intimate friendship is reserved for those who are more equally yoked with our heart's desires, goals, and purposes. You first need to define what your heart's desire is in pleasing God, and then choose friends that will help you express what is in your heart.

---

[9] Webster, Noah., *Letters to a Young Gentleman Commencing His Education*, 1823 (cited in *Rudiments of America's Christian History and Government: A Student Handbook*, by Rosalie J. Slater and Verna M. Hall, Foundation for American Christian Education, San Francisco, CA, 1968), page 77.

Key Ingredients in True Friends

When one builds a friendship, what kind of characteristics should be seen? How do we know that one is a true friend? Well, consider some of the following verses of Scripture on some basic aspects of friendship; taken from Larry Tomczak's book *Let's Talk About Sex,* which sets forth true friendship as God's alternative for dating.[10]

(1) Friends are **Unique**
"A man of many friends comes to ruin." - Proverbs 18:24
You will not have many true friends. In your entire life, you may not ever have more than 10 or 15 really close friends. It isn't possible or practical. Thus, the first characteristic we could list about friends is that they are unique. They are unique to you, and in that way, special.

(2) Friends are **Servants**
"Greater love has no one than this, that one lay down his life for his friends." - John 15:13 (NAS)
In other words, a friend is a servant. He or she is willing to sacrifice whatever is necessary for your benefit. Inconvenience does not exist between friends. It doesn't matter when it is, they will be there if needed.

(3) Friends **Know You**
"I have called you friends, for all that I have heard from my Father I have made known to you." - John 15:15 (RSV)
A friend allows you to know them. Friends really know you as well, the way you really are, and not the way you pretend to be in certain situations. A friend cuts through the mask. You can really confide in a friend and discuss the most serious things in your life. This is the level at which friendship is true fellowship.

---

[10] Tomczak, Larry., *Let's Talk About Sex*, (Vine Books, 1987), page 78, 108-115.

(4) Friends are **Loyal**

"A friend loves at all times, and a brother is born with adversity" -
- Proverbs 17:17 (RSV)

Friends are loyal. They are with you in good and bad times. They do not leave when the going gets rough or when you get rough. They are not just friends when you are in a good mood! This loyalty does not mean that they will ignore your faults and worship you. It means they will stand by you, even if you are wrong and need correction.

(5) Friends give **Good Advice**

"Oil and perfume make the heart glad, so a man's counsel is sweet to his friend." - Proverbs 27:9 (NAS)

A friend gives you good and timely advice. They know what to say at the right time, and it can save you embarrassment and headaches. The advice can be trusted because you know they are looking out for your best interest.

(6) Friends **Confront**

"Faithful are the wounds of a friend; profuse are the kisses of an enemy." - Proverbs 27:6 (RSV)

True friends are willing to correct you. They say what is right no matter what you think, or how you argue with them. They lift you up when you are about to fall. They correct you when you are wrong. What a blessing to have this kind of a friend!

(7) Friends **Encourage**

"For the despairing man there should be kindness from his friend"
- Job 6:14 (NAS)

A friend encourages. When you are down, a true friend will encourage you to take courage and not get so depressed. Encouragement can come in many ways. It can be direct, or it can be more subtle, but a true friend will put courage in you when you need it, and this is true kindness. What a joy to have a friend like this!

(8) Friends are **Honest**

"Iron sharpens iron; so a man sharpens the countenance of his friend as in water face answers face so the heart of man to man." - Proverbs 27:17,19

A friend is also honest. One who shares his heart face to face is honest with you. There are no put-ons. It also may hurt, because honesty also forms growth in you. You grow through iron sharpening iron, and honesty clashes with reality.

(9) Friends **Respect You**

"As a mad man casts firebrands, arrows, and death, so is the man that deceives his neighbor, and says, Am not I in sport?" - Proverbs 26:18-19

A friend does not play a joke that might injure you. A friend always shows respect. Teasing and joking to injure one's emotional feelings is not characteristic of a true friend. In fact, it is more like an enemy. With a true friend there is respect, not deception. Respect means someone will speak the truth and you can trust their intentions.

(10) Friends are **Trustworthy**

"He who repeats a matter alienates a friend"
- Proverbs 17:9 (RSV)

Finally, you can trust a friend. He will not gossip about you or spread rumors that hurt you. He will tell you first, face to face. Even if it means the truth will hurt, yet be for your good, he will tell you face to face.

What are we to say, then? A true friend is one who is *unique*. A friend *sacrifices* for your benefit. A friend *knows you*. A friend is *loyal* and will not leave when it gets rough. A friend will *confront* and correct you when you are wrong, and *encourage* you when you are down. A friend is *honest* with you, sharing heart to heart. A friend *respects* you whether you are right or wrong, and thus you can trust that individual.

These characteristics should first be cultivated between you and the Lord, and then with your parents. What a blessing to have a relationship with your father and mother with these characteristics! Then, you have the platform to form these with other adults and young people in the team ministry atmosphere spoken of earlier.

Levels of Friendship

Bill Gothard examines the levels of friendship and gives us an excellent outline of what to expect when forming friends. This can serve as a process that we can ponder when forming true friends. Let us examine his outline:[11]

1. Acquaintance - this is based on occasional contacts where you have the freedom to ask general questions. We all can learn to ask the kinds of questions to help us be friendly in these situations when meeting people.

2. Casual Friendship - this is based on common interests, activities and concerns. We have the freedom to ask specific questions of one another's opinions, ideas, wishes and goals. This type of friendship helps us to get to know someone else with an attitude of concern about them and not just ourselves.

3. Close Friendship and Fellowship - this is based on mutual life goals. We have the freedom to suggest mutual projects and plans to reach those goals. We can be creative in helping friends achieve their goals rather than just talking about them.

4. Intimate Friendship and Fellowship - this is based on commitment to develop each other's character. We have the freedom to correct one another and be honest. We can even begin to see the causes for character problems in one another, and help to correct them.

As one can readily see, these steps take time and effort. As we form these kinds of friendships with those on a team, we are learning to form the kinds of friendships needed in marriage. When done in a group, there is no emotional pressure, no intimacy with boy-girl relationships in pairs. Instead, we learn to be in close fellowship with

---

[11] Gothard, Bill., *Discerning Levels of Friendship*, Institute in Basic Youth Conflicts, page 167.

each other as a group, with only a certain number with whom we are really close. In this way, we best prepare for our future lifelong practice of mutual friendship with our spouse.

A Voluntary Covenant of Purity

"But Daniel purposed in his heart that he would not defile himself." - Daniel 1:8a

Most commentators agree that Daniel was probably about 16 years old when taken to Babylon. In a different country, faced with countless temptations, he stood strong. We have all heard of the great stories involving Daniel's strength and consistency. Why did he have this as a teenager? It was because he voluntarily purposed in his heart to stay pure. Though the context was obedience to God's Law in the area of health, it can speak to us in any area.

Today young people can rise to the occasion and agree to covenant together for purity. We can covenant to build true friends rather than dating pairs. We can covenant to be a demonstration of the keeping power of God for His glory!

One of the keys to a covenant of purity is to build fences far enough away from the cliff so that we do not fall over. The goal of the Christian life is not to come as close to the edge as possible without falling off. When we live like this, one small mistake and we fall off! We should not be asking the question "how far can I go toward sensuality without getting into trouble", but rather "how close can I get with God?" That is the purpose of a covenant of purity. It builds the fences far enough away from danger to keep us safe and help us maintain boundaries. The following covenant is an example of what can be agreed upon in any group of young people or adults, from the natural family to the church.

A Covenant of Purity in the Home

The first team is the home, and the first place where true friends are built is the home as well. It is also the first place where a covenant of purity should be practiced. One of the key ways in which a father can build the protection necessary for maintaining purity is to "court his daughter" and have a "man to man" relationship with his son. When no father exists in the home, the mother must ask for God's grace to fulfill this role, together with the male examples of exemplary fathers, elders and teens within the church. Included would be at least the following:

1. *Starting early* - It is necessary to begin this kind of relationship at a very young age. Girls need the security of being loved, and boys need the security of responsibility and solid leadership. By five years of age, it should be standard practice for Dad to spend quality time alone with each of his children. Mom usually spends great quantities of time alone with them simply by the lifestyle she leads. But, if that is not the case, then special times should be arranged with her as well.

2. *Natural affection* - It is important for young people to see their parents going out of their way to demonstrate their love - verbally, socially, and physically. Verbal praise is extremely rewarding in a young person's heart and spirit. Social praise involves being interested in what the children are interested in, including their talents (whether it be athletics, or some other hobby or interest), as well saying positive things about them in public. Physical praise through natural affection is also very necessary. Frequent embraces, hugs and kisses, become the normal part of family life between parents and children.

3. *Building a Relationship* - As a young person grows older, a solid relationship can be built so that it can truly be said a teenager's best friend is his or her Mom and Dad. They can talk about anything, and I mean anything, without being made to feel insecure or unusual.

One can only imagine the tension when a teenager has become pregnant, or gotten someone pregnant, and has to break the news to his or her parents as if telling a stranger. Many simply opt for abortion and murder the pre born child in hopes of eliminating the consequences of sin. If the relationships had been built, the chances of the above situation grow very slim. Activities such as going out to dinner alone where Dad opens doors and treats his daughter like the lady she really is, together with special times alone with his son, become pillars and memories hard to erase in a moment of temptation.

Bill Gothard, in his excellent booklet, *Establishing Biblical Standards of Courtship*, gives an example of a father's covenant with his daughter and son in which they mutually agree to preserve their purity until marriage. The daughter or son agrees to submit to parental consent and the father agrees to protect his child's purity and help discern their life's mate. A covenant such as this is, of course, the natural external expression of a solid relationship built some years earlier.

Parents should be the first to be consulted when a son or daughter feels that they may have found the one God has called them to marry; not just because it is the pattern of Biblical truth (as we shall see in the next lesson), but because it is usually your best friend that you tell first!

A Covenant of Purity in the Church and School

The church and school need to extend, confirm and help protect the convictions and practices of the Christian home. Thus, the covenant of purity between a daughter and son becomes the basis for extending this into team ministry in the context of the church and Christian school (which is the true Children's Church).

One way in which to practice this covenant of purity, in addition to situations of ministry, are special activities where a group of teens, their parents and several other adults can conduct an "etad." An "etad" is simply a date spelled backwards. The term was first coined by the late Walter Trobisch who taught it as a replacement for the dating pattern. An "etad" is simply a group activity where adults and youth practice treating one another with honor and respect. It combines the elements of team ministry and building friendships. The characteristics we have developed include:

1. In the context of ministry (on the way to the location or on the way home,) we do a special activity as a group. This might include going out to dinner at a restaurant or some other activity such as

bowling, biking, hiking or touring an area. The purpose is to consciously and purposefully treat others with respect.

2. The boys open doors, help the girls be seated, treating them with respect and honor. The girls respond accordingly; and all in all, we are practicing honoring one another in a special way. We review our "covenant of purity" and make a special effort to emphasize the points we have agreed upon during a specific activity.

3. Memories of these events are planted deep within. There is no reason why the principles in this book must be dull, boring, or hard to keep. When elevated within the context of ministry, they are exciting and helpful. As you ponder the covenant of purity that concludes this lesson, let it sink deep within as the replacement for a practice which has never really worked, and let it give you vision for the way you can creatively apply these principles in whatever situation you find yourself.

The following covenant is an example of what can be agreed upon in any group of youth and adults from the natural family to the church extension of such a team.

A Team Covenant of Purity

Attitudes of the Team:

1. We give attention to all members of the team, though we realize that some will be closer to certain members. Each member is important and has gifts to share.

2. We are open and honest in our communication. Our topics are clean and pure and lift up our purpose of ministry.

3. We demonstrate in our attitudes an intense desire for God; His purposes and His holiness. We help one another avoid any kind of distraction that would take away from our purpose.

4. We maintain personal standards in dress, appearance, gestures and manners of conduct so that we demonstrate our desire to bring attention to God and the character He has built into our lives.

Actions of the Team:

5. We avoid all situations where a boy and girl would be alone together as a pair.

6. We encourage natural brother-sister affection, but avoid any actions such as holding hands, embracing, putting arms around each other, leaning or hanging on one another. Though these actions may be normal for natural family affections at times, they are not appropriate for team ministry extensions.

7. We will avoid, with foresight and planning, all situations and environments in vans, cars, planes or other places where a guy and giirl would be sitting together at night in order to avoid all appearance of evil.

8. We will fulfill our respective roles as men and women. We wish for the guys to lead, protect and demonstrate courtesy such as opening doors, carrying heavy equipment and watching out for the safety of the girls. We wish for the girls to be respectful and work with the details, often willing to do the "behind the scenes" work if it means encouraging one of the guys to accept more leadership.

9. Our conduct will always reflect the seriousness with which we intend to fulfill God's purposes, knowing when to cease from humorous and more light actions.

10. Whether an adult is around or not, we will voluntarily endeavor to maintain ethical standards in host homes, ministry at altars and other such places, avoiding any appearance of improper actions, even if encouraged by others who do not hold the same standards.

As we agree together, voluntarily, God will honor our desires and together we can keep the enemy from defiling our vision and ministry. We will also protect one another so that we can bring the greatest character and lifestyle into our future marriages. In this way we will help each other to fulfill the highest calling God has on each life.

May God help us prepare to restore the foundations of many generations!

Lesson Seven

COURTSHIP: PREPARATION FOR MARRIAGE

When the Pharisees came to Jesus wondering what his views were on divorce, they were shocked to find Jesus so strong on adhering to the Law of God in the Old Testament. The Pharisees had warped God's standards and replaced them with their own traditions. They had exchanged God's Law for their own where one could get a divorce for just about any reason at all. This was a disgrace to God's standards, and also meant a lack of respect toward women. When Jesus gave the answer to their question below, everyone got the clear picture that marriage was serious; so important in fact that one had to understand that *God* was the One actually joining two people together!

> *"Have you not read, that he which made them at the beginning made them male and female, and said, for this cause shall a man leave father and mother, and shall cleave to his wife, and they shall be one flesh? Wherefore they are no more twain, but one flesh. What therefore God has joined together, let not man put asunder."* - Matthew 19:4-6

Jesus' disciples were shocked at this answer! In fact, upon hearing of God's standards of purity, and the holiness of marriage before God and His Law they responded:

> *"If the case of the man be so with his wife, it is not good to marry."* - Matthew 19:10

In other words, if the standard is this high, it is too difficult, so why bother! You may be asking yourself the same question. You may be saying to yourself, "if I give up the dating process, and move in team ministry within my family, church and other kinds of ministry teams, trusting and waiting for God to bring my future mate into my path, I may never get married!" Many often ask, "if we can't date, how do we ever get married? How will I ever get to know someone if I don't spend time alone with them? If I am always in groups, when do I ever get to know someone more seriously?"

These and other questions are legitimate. That is why this lesson has been written. One needs to understand God's Law and how one got married according to God's standards. Once understanding the standards of God, it is time to *trust God*. If we can trust God to save us for eternity, we can trust Him to bring our mate to us at the perfect time! If God can initiate His love and grace toward us, and also give us the ability to respond, He can certainly bring our mate toward us, and give them the ability to respond!

Without this kind of trust and understanding of God's Law, we have no absolute basis upon which to reason and apply the patterns and principles today. Courtship is the legitimate time to seriously consider whether the other individual is the one God has called for you to marry. It is the beginning of "pairing up," yet with the walls and standards necessary to minimize the hurt while pondering God's will if the individual is not the one for you. It is God's best for you not to ever have to date, and only court the one God has designed for you for life.

Mistakes will be made, but when they are made within the boundaries of God's righteous standards, we are free from the traps of emotional, sensual and passionate involvement prior to marriage! The important thing to remember is the fact that the standards, cautions and all that we have talked about is for the primary purpose of getting married to the one God intended for you. We should all desire for *God* to join us together in marriage rather than our own feelings, emotions or lustful desires!

Courtship

"COURTSHIP, n. The act of soliciting favor. 2. The act of wooing in love; solicitation of a woman to marriage. 3. Civility; elegance of manners." - Webster's 1828 Dictionary

The word courtship involves two clear meanings. First of all it is the stage where we seriously prepare for marriage. Second, it deals with law - a court - testing the evidence as to whether two individuals are called together by God through the discernment of manners and standards of elegance. Courtship is not the legal time to arouse passions - for that would be against pure manners, and would be no test at all. It would also not be civil. However, it is the time to seriously consider one person who may be your mate for life.

To court a woman is similar to what one used to call "the suitor." Webster uses it as a synonym for courting. Like one who petitions a court for a just claim, so a man petitions for the hand of a woman. Thus, when speaking of courtship, we are speaking of a very lawful and serious concentration of a man and woman in relation to marriage. It means serious intentions. This is the only time "pairing up" is within Biblical principles, yet very different from dating.

Dating concentrates on non-serious passionate involvement, or the careless spending of emotions that often end in separation, rejection and heartache; only to be repeated again and again. Courtship is not to be redefined as "lawful dating" where people simply go from one person to the other "seriously pondering" marriage. Courtship is the time when Biblical betrothal is entered, where potential engagement takes place that is as solid a commitment as marriage itself. It is the time when God is drawing a man and a woman together to consider marriage seriously.

It is the time to test, prove and confirm the sense of God's drawing as a couple bring it to court in order to fully establish the truth of God's call. The courtship time is where at least two or three witnesses will confirm that indeed God is calling two individuals to become one and married for life. Since both are serious, the witnesses can never injure them, only help them.

Who would want to make a mistake in such a serious endeavor? Like the Pharisees and others today are accustomed to thinking; if marriage is not serious, and merely the extension of the dating pattern (easy divorce or breaking up,) then either throw out courting or throw out marriage!

Before we walk ourselves through the courtship stage and its characteristics, we need to pause and consider God's instructions regarding preparation for marriage. In a sense, these are God's instructions on preparing for the courting stage. If these are not understood and practiced, courtship is usually entered too quickly and thus mistakes are made and heartache results.

God's Law of the Dower

"And Laban had two daughters: the name of the elder was Leah, and the name of the younger was Rachel ... And Jacob loved Rachel; and said, I will serve thee seven years for Rachel thy daughter.... And Jacob served seven years for Rachel: and they seemed unto him but a few days, for the love he had to her."
- Genesis 29:16, 18, 20

Jacob was serious about marrying Rachel. However, he was *not* prepared. One of the first preparations in Scripture for marriage is the existence of a dower. Jacob worked seven years to have enough for a dower for Rachel. Actually, it was far more than he needed, since most authorities feel the dower was usually about three years' wages.[12] However, his love for Rachel was so strong he was willing to work seven years and give her a large dower.

A dower is defined by Webster as:

"DOWER. 1. That portion of the lands or tenements of a man which his widow enjoys during her life, after the death of her husband. 2. The property which a woman brings to her husband in marriage. 3. The gift of a husband for a wife. 4. Endowment; gift."
- Webster's 1828 Dictionary

---

[12] Rushdoony, Rousas J., *Institutes of Biblical Law*, The Craig Press, 1973, pages 176-177.

We see here that Webster defines the word Scripturally and helps us identify several key characteristics of its meaning. Simply put, a dower involves both *time* and *property*. In other words, before marriage ought to be seriously considered, the Bible gives us real wisdom in stating that both husband and wife should <u>wait</u> until they are able to bring a significant amount of <u>property</u> into the marriage.

Does this imply that both need to be financially rich? Financial security is important, and getting married in debt brings great strain upon a marriage, but the implication here is far more than mere external riches. Property is both internal and external. To acquire both takes time and one must be willing to wait in order to be ready.

The practice of two individuals getting married "in love," yet with no preparation of waiting until both the internal property of mature character and the external property of security has been acquired is certainly unwise at the very least. In Jacob's case, he worked seven extra years in order to bring property into the marriage. It is obvious that the property he brought to the marriage was both in his character as well as in economic resources. What a blessing to wait! What love to be willing to sacrifice time for a better foundation!

Being willing to spend the time necessary to mature in character and build secure resources means that *respect* for each other is being brought into the marriage as well. Getting married wasn't the ultimate goal since that was only the beginning. Quick marriages out of emotional desperation due to a lack of security in character only magnifies the insecurity by at least a factor of two!

Notice that both husband and wife brought a dower to their marriage. The groom brought the dowry as a demonstration of his love, but more importantly to protect his wife and his children's inheritance. If one married without a dower, then it was not considered a true and lawful marriage, but it was considered "concubinage," or a form of slavery.[13] There was no protection for the woman should the man die. There was no inheritance left for her or her children either. Without a dower a woman would remain dependent upon the church, or worse yet, the state.

---

[13] *Ibid.*, page 176.

Thus, we see that the dower had two purposes for the woman - protection against the death of her husband or the death of her marriage - divorce. It even protected her before marriage against being raped or seduced by a man and losing her virginity. If one lost their virginity, the chances of marriage became less likely. However, the Bible declares that the man who seduces a woman must give a dower to the girl as if he married her (see Exodus 22:16-17; Deuteronomy 22:28-29.) It was also an inheritance for the children should the man die or divorce her, or anything happen that should put the children in jeopardy.

A dower was also brought by the woman into the marriage. It was usually given to her by her father, who since her birth had been preparing her with an inheritance for this special day in her life. This was in keeping with the fact that the Bible places special emphasis upon the bride's family and especially her father to prepare ahead of time for the marriage of his daughter.

Time; the test of Character and Financial Security

Part of the reason for the dower was to affirm the father's role in voicing both his opinion as well as preparing a financial inheritance for his daughter. Why should the woman be so doubly protected by both her husband to be and her father? Receiving a dower from both sources lays quite a solid foundation economically in the new home. It also provides a clear check on quick marriages. This check is the necessary ingredient of *time.*

It takes time to discern the will of God. It takes time to build internal maturity. Though some marriages in the Bible involved youth in their teens, the age of adulthood (involving an ability to go to war) was 20.[14] Throughout history men and women usually get married no earlier than 20 or 21. And there is no stigma for one to wait much longer than this. Taking the time necessary for *you* to prepare is both wise and prudent. Time allows the father and the future husband to build a financial dower. It also allows both the bride and groom to mature in character and the demonstration of responsibility.

---

[14] See Numbers 1 and following for the 20 year old standard.

Dating vs. Courtship

A woman is to be in submission to either her father or her husband. This does not mean that she must always obey her father once she is on her own, but it does mean a respect and honor that involves an attitude of submission. A woman has the ultimate veto in any marriage proposal and is not less than equal to men. Submission means more than respect for those in authority, it also means one is protected. As the laws in America have changed, women have not been "liberated", but instead a woman's security and protection has been weakened. Women are now more exploited than ever before because of their lack of protection. As this has occurred, we have had less respect for the element of *time* and consequently have lost discernment.

Also, when men are deceived and in disobedience to God's Law, they often exploit women as well. They are the ones who abandon women and their children. The statistics on "dead beat Dads" tell the story of modern America's rebellion against God's Law and the lack of respect toward *time* that a mature commitment requires. Rushing into marriage can lead to rushing out of marriage. If one is unwilling to properly prepare, then the foundation is weak and it can lead to a loss of security.

The Law of the Dower provides a protection of a woman's legitimate rights. Since she bears the children, she is doubly protected. A dower, then, is one of the safest protections against non-serious marriages! If a man needs to work hard to bring a good dower into the marriage, he will think twice about simply wasting it through fornication and other shallow commitments. If a father has worked his whole life for an inheritance at his daughter's wedding, he will surely think twice before giving his positive consent to the marriage. This is the positive role that a respect for *time* has on a potential marriage.

As a closing note, it is interesting that our word wedding actually means the "wed or bride price" and refers to the Biblical dower. One only needs to look at the scene today to see the wisdom of God's Word. Most often people get married due to their emotional attachments that grow from a dating pattern of behavior. Thus, emotions are involved before sound thinking.

Usually marriages today begin on a very unstable economic base, are rushed ahead of their time, and thus poverty (internal, or spiritual, as well as external, or financial) becomes the standard foundation of the new home. This breeds discontent, and often births bitterness in the woman as well as the man. If a man does not have the character to begin his home on the right foot, then he ought to wait, and a woman ought to think more seriously about whether he is really the man for her. Are you willing to pass the first test of being ready for courtship? This test is a willingness to wait for the right *time*.

Bringing the Internal Property
of Character into a Marriage

In addition to the test of time, especially as it relates to the external preparation for marriage with the financial dower, we also have clear instruction about the internal preparation for marriage that is needed as well - maturity or character. Consider the first couple of the human race - Adam and Eve. God arranged the marriage directly. There was no dating, only clear courtship and marriage.

Adam demonstrated his character before God brought Eve to him. This was a protection for Eve. After all, who else was she to marry? Thus, what we see God doing is actually preparing Adam for marriage. Imagine that! The instructions given to Adam before Eve was created, in addition to setting forth clear principles for life in general, were also to help him prepare for marriage!

The Character of the Man

> *"And the Lord God took the man, and put him into the garden of Eden to dress it and keep it." - Genesis 2:15*

The following are some of the key characteristics, illustrating Adam's practice of Biblical principles in his life, that caused him to be prepared to marry Eve. These become a pattern for us that can help every young woman begin to discern the internal character qualities of her future mate.

1. Adam understood his *calling* in God (Genesis 1:26-28).

106

It was general, to be sure, but he did understand why he was created, and what his calling was in the earth. It is important that a man know his calling and duty before God before getting married. How can he lead his family if he has no idea where he is going? How can a woman help a man fulfill his calling if he has no understanding of his calling before God? Thus, every woman should expect that her husband would bring clear vision into the marriage, and *demonstrate the desire to walk in his calling before getting married.*

2. Adam was also a good _worker_ (Genesis 2:15).

He exercised both character and stewardship in the garden. If a man cannot work hard while single, he won't work hard when married. As we mentioned before, this trait should be so strong that even if he has no property or inheritance to bring into the marriage, he would be willing to work for an extended time while single to obtain one. *A demonstration of working hard is part of a man's stewardship for his new home.*

3. Adam exercised *responsibility* (Genesis 2:16-17).

This involved obedience to God's instructions (self-government) and understanding the consequences of disobedience (sowing and reaping.) Adam had to understand both responsibility and accountability to authority. One of the saddest commentaries today involves marriages where the man takes no responsibility for the condition of his home (wife and children) economically, spiritually or socially. What is worse is that the woman did not discern this in his life prior to marriage. *A man ought to demonstrate a measure of responsibility in situations prior to marriage.*

4. Adam understood his _need_ for a helpmate (Genesis 2:18-25).

A man's understanding of a woman is essential before getting married. If there is no appreciation of his need for a helpmeet then a woman can become practically a servant, or worse yet, a slave to be bossed around, give him sex when his passions are aroused, and be used and abused. If a man doesn't particularly desire to be married, or see his need for help, cooperation and covenant with his wife, his willingness to get married is for the wrong reason. Understanding his need will involve joint reasoning (or the principle of Sovereignty) to iron out problems (without any form of dictatorship), and a covenant commitment for life based on internal unity of ideas and principles. *If a man doesn't demonstrate a desire to discuss and reason, including other points of view, he is not ready for marriage.*

5. Adam exercised *creativity* in his walk with God (Genesis 2:19).

He named the animals, both out of obedience but also in an act of dominion over creation, personally fulfilling his calling (Genesis 1:28). If a woman sees no personal walk with God (individuality) in a man, no clear relationship with God, but simply attention upon her or a tolerance toward spiritual things, there is danger ahead. Interestingly enough, the word bridegroom in the Hebrew means "circumcised" and indicates a circumcised heart and walk with God. *Any man that does not demonstrate a heart for God before marriage is not likely to be a spiritual leader in marriage.*

The Character of the Woman

> *"Who can find a virtuous woman? for her price is far above rubies."* - Proverbs 31:10

The virtuous woman described in Proverbs 31 is a picture of what any man should look for in a bride. Far from what most people think, the Bible paints no picture of a dull, sullen, lazy, slavish woman who simply lives beneath the foot of a man. This woman has characteristics every bit as noble as the man. God always deals with co-equality between men and women, but also distinguishes their functions. Let us take a look:

1. This woman knows her *calling* in God.

Like Eve, she sees her primary responsibility as one that serves her family. As the man is called to extend the dominion of the Kingdom of God in the earth, so she is to extend that same dominion within her home as her first priority. *If a woman does not demonstrate taking care of her own family's needs as well as the poor and needy around her, she is not ready for marriage* (Proverbs 31:20-22).

2. A virtuous woman is known for her *diligence*.

108

She does not eat the "bread of idleness," gossiping and spending hours simply trifling about matters which mean little. She exercises character and stewardship as well as the man but in different spheres. She cares for her family, and works in the house from early in the morning until the evening. *A woman that demonstrates no ability or desire to manage a home business or some kind of productive skill is not ready for marriage* (Proverbs 31:15-19, 27).

3. This woman can be *trusted.*

Her word is law, and you can count on her. She exercises self-government and understands the consequences of her actions (sowing and reaping). She can bring a task from start to completion. *A man ought to be careful of a woman who does not demonstrate trustworthiness morally or financially, for she is not fully ready for marriage* (Proverbs 31:11-12).

4. A wife sees her *need* for a husband to protect her.

This protection is spiritual through her submissive attitude, social through her own work in extending her family and its influence, and physical by being under her husband's protective influence. She understands her role of speaking wisdom into the marriage relationship (reasoning) yet in covenant for her own protection. Thus, *a woman who seeks no protection, is full of pride and individualism, who puts careers ahead of home and self-glorification ahead of her children, is not prepared for marriage* (Proverbs 31:28).

5. A virtuous woman exercises *inner beauty* in her walk with God.

This is what makes a woman, in essence, virtuous. This means that she has a walk with God internally and independently (individuality) that is beautiful to behold. She is more concerned with inner beauty than external beauty. Those women who prepare for marriage by making themselves showboats of the latest fashions are simply luxury dolls with little internal character. Consider the fact that this woman expresses her love for God and internal beauty by speaking in wisdom, with her works praising her in the gates. This is no idle homemaker who submits to her husband with no thinking. *If a woman does not place a priority on inner beauty that is worthy of praise but instead focuses on pleasing people through external appearance alone, she is not ready for marriage* (Proverbs 31:10,23-31).

In summary, doesn't it make sense to follow the Biblical admonitions in preparation for marriage? Let us not simply bring external dowers into our marriages. Let's bring the internal ones as well. In this way the influence of the restored homes of the next generation will uproot the enemy in every area where he has a stronghold.

Consider the following New Testament passage of Scripture which describes the same attributes above but in a different way. Let us restore the highest preparation possible for God's plan to restore His Kingdom!

> *"Likewise, you wives, be in subjection to your own husbands... while they behold your chaste conversation coupled with fear. Whose adorning let it not be that outward adorning of plaiting the hair, and of wearing of gold, or putting on of apparel; but let it be the hidden man of the heart, in that which is not corruptible, even the ornament of a meek and quiet spirit, which is in the sight of God of great price... Likewise, you husbands, dwell with them according to knowledge, giving honor unto the wife, as unto the weaker vessel, and as being heirs together of the grace of life, that your prayers be not hindered."*
> - 1 Peter 3:1-4,7

Parental Consent

Probably one of the greatest weaknesses of the dating pattern in America and around the world is the absence of the proper role of parents in preparing to help guide the marriages of their children. While the absence of responsible preparation (time, finances and character) are obvious to all, the absence of the role of the parent is less noticed and discussed. While it is true that in Bible days the parents, (especially the bride) had quite a bit of authority regarding the marriage of their daughter, it is only a myth that the Bible instructed parents to choose mates for their children without their consent.

"Then Laban and Bethuel answered and said, the thing proceedeth from the Lord; we cannot speak unto thee bad or good. Behold, Rebekah is before thee, take her, and go, and let her be thy master's son's wife, as the Lord hath spoken." - Genesis 24:50-51

"And they called Rebekah, and said unto her, Wilt thou go with this man? And she said, I will go."
- Genesis 24:58

The Biblical pattern was that the parents of the bride had more authority in consent than the parents of the groom. This is because a woman is in subjection to her father's protection. She should welcome this. The man is to leave his father and mother and form a new family as the head of his home. The key point in all of this is that there is a role the parents play for the protection of the new couple. Let us see positively why the Bible has this as a pattern.

"... at the mouth of two witnesses, or at the mouth of three witnesses, shall the matter be established." - Deuteronomy 19:15b

Although this verse deals specifically with the context of determining sin like a court of law, it also deals in principle with the determining of direction and God's will. It is wisdom from the Lord. It means greater safety in making important decisions. What more important decision can you think of than the lifelong commitment of marriage?

"Where no counsel is, the people fall: but in the multitude of counselors there is safety." - Proverbs 11:14

> *"Without counsel purposes are disappointed: but in the multitude of counselors they are established."* - Proverbs 15:22

The question we must ask is: who should be the counselors in relation to a confirmation about getting married? First of all, the Bible requires us to honor our parents. Without question, they ought to be the first witnesses. Quite logically, other individuals older than we - who are experienced, who know us, have led us, such as church elders and other respected individuals in our lives - should also be included.

The context of the New Testament suggests that in marriage matters generally the elders do play a role, (see 1st Timothy 5). Now consider this verse of Scripture also:

> *"If we receive the witness of men, the witness of God is greater... He that believeth on the Son of God hath the witness in himself.."* - I John 5:9-10

Now that the Holy Spirit resides within each of us who are believers, we have even less of an excuse to be totally dependent upon external confirmations from others. The Law of God regarding confirmation has not been removed, we still need the confirmation, and it would be foolish to do without it, but since we have the Holy Spirit within us, *we must hear God for ourselves.* This is our first priority.

Thus, God must first speak to you personally and your potential bride or groom - separately. The witness must be in both of you independently before the Lord. Then, as you seek counsel and confirmation from your parents, church leaders and others, you wisely seek their advice for your own protection. In other words, your personal witness comes first. Then the second witness involves your parents. The third witness would fall to church elders or other respected individuals in your life. *Let your marriage be established in the agreement of two or three witnesses* and you will have a greater chance of understanding God's will in such a major decision.

What if your parents do not know the Lord? Or worse, what if you feel you could not trust their counsel for some reason regarding getting married? I believe that the Bible tells us that we should seek counsel from our parents on the basis of honoring them. You honor them by asking their advice and by *truly considering what they say seriously.*

Church leaders and other respected individuals take a secondary place but are also to be honored. If you are under age, still living at home and dependent upon your parents, then you should obey them and wait until you are on your own before making independent decisions. Don't leave in order to get married, be willing to wait. Even if you are on your own, you should still weigh the counsel you receive from others quite seriously.

However, I do not believe that the Lord commands you to follow the counsel of others, no matter what it is. The greatest witness is that within you, from the Holy Spirit. If you neglect seriously considering the counsel or disobey while under your parent's authority you can count on some negative consequences. Walk in the wisdom that God has given in His Word.

The Process of Courtship

Now that we have considered the meaning of courtship, the Biblical preparation of a dower (time, finances and character,) and the need for confirmation first from your parents and then the church and other respected individuals, let us now follow a step-by-step process from team ministry to courtship and on to the wedding day.

We will use one of the most beautifully outlined pictures of one's preparation for marriage in the Bible - the story of Isaac and Rebekah. Let us follow it and highlight the steps that form a pattern we can use for our wisdom. The pattern is not legalistic or meant to be followed exactly, since every situation is somewhat different. However, in principle it is an authoritative guide for us to follow.

Prayer

> *"The Lord God of heaven, which took me from my father's house, and from the land of my kindred, and which space unto me, and that swore unto me, saying*

> *unto thy seed will I give this land; he shall send his*
> *angel before thee, and thou shalt take a wife unto my*
> *son from thence. "* - Genesis 24:7

Our story begins with a prayer from Abraham, father of his son Isaac. Courtship always flows out of a life of prayer. The Bible even says that a life of prayer and fasting can keep one from fornication and prepare you for a life of purity before marriage (see 1st Corinthians 9:25-27 and Jeremiah 5:7.) Your prayers, and the prayers of your parents in relation to God's eternal purposes and call upon your life are a key to having God bring in your path the individual He has called for you to marry. This is indeed the first step.

This step should begin in earnest the moment you find yourself the least bit interested in the opposite sex. From that point until marriage, form a private, confidential prayer team with your parents for your future marriage partner. Then, let it progress to prayer and fasting as you get older and more ready to seriously consider God's choice for your life. I feel it is wise not to seriously begin to attempt to discern God's mate until you are at least 18 years old.

In the typology of Scripture, Isaac is like Christ, Rebekah is a picture of the church and Eleanor the servant like the Holy Spirit. Abraham is Father God. You see, it is the Father who has sought a wife for His Son, Jesus. The servant sent out by Abraham to find a wife for Isaac is like the Holy Spirit who has been searching and preparing the church throughout the ages for the great marriage that is to take place. Thus, our story, according to the Bible, is on two levels, the spiritual and the natural.[15]

God's Call in the Midst of Service (or Team Ministry)

> *"And the damsel was very fair to look upon, a virgin,*
> *neither had any man known her; and she went down to*
> *the well, and filled her pitcher, and came up. "* -
> Genesis 24:16

---

[15] see Galatians 4:21-31.

We see that Rebekah was preparing herself for the Holy Spirit to speak to her regarding her future mate. Eleanor comes to the well, and finds Rebekah ministering through service. Rebekah did not go out aggressively and seek a husband. She did not flirt until one fell into her trap through seduction. She did what she had always been doing. In her case, it was drawing water from the city well for her family and in type drawing from the well of spiritual life.

We need to understand that the well was the social place in those days. It would be like going to the market today. Everyone talked at the well. It was the place where you caught up on the news of what was happening to others nearby. Communication was not as easy as it is today. Thus, it was in the place of normal social intercourse that Rebekah would notice her future husband. Thus, as Rebekah was ministering in a social context (internal team ministry in the context of her family,) she was ready to receive the call of God for her future mate.

Isaac, many miles away, is also preparing through ministry. He is in the field, working as usual, but also near a well. He was drawing on the same water of life that Rebekah was, though they did not know each other and certainly had no knowledge that they were called together. In fact, it is stated that Isaac was in prayer in the field (probably a habit) toward evening. He was not out dating. He was not out flirting around with as many women as possible to see which one was right for him. Women are not used cars to be tried before purchase.

Isaac was coming from this context of ministry, and since society at this time was mostly agricultural, he was working on his father's farm, (see Genesis 24:62-63).

Pledge and Proposal

> *"And it came to pass, as the camels had done drinking, that the man took a golden earring of half a shekel weight, and two bracelets for her hands of ten shekels weight of gold."* - Genesis 24:22

115

Our next step involves the beginning of the courtship stage. Here the servant gives to Rebekah a token of the dower. This is serious business now. This would be like a man feeling the call of God toward a woman and willingly saying in his heart that she could be the one for him, willing to make it known to her, but also willing to let God (Eleazar) work in her heart first.

This is a step of God's internal call upon the man as well as the woman - but still independently from each other. As you minister, you begin to notice the characteristics (internal and external) of the preparation of God in another individual. You are attracted. It is not merely external beauty, it is an internal call from God. There is no other way to explain it.

All the practice at hearing God's voice and moving with others in ministry now has a different ring to it. However, though you are willing to offer the treasure of your heart, you take it to God and wait for Him to speak to her as well. This is the first part of a pledge and proposal to God that is yet to be made real to the other individual.

Confirmation: The Second and Third Witness

"And the damsel ran, and told them of her mother's house these things." - Genesis 4:28

The first response, in principle, of a man or woman who hears the voice and call of God through discerning His will, is to present the case to their family - or mother and father! What a relationship she must have had with them. At the first sign of God moving seriously in determining one's mate - having kept herself a virgin all these years - was to share it with her parents. This is indeed a step of parental confirmation. Much takes place in discussion here, as all of them question and hear from this strange servant (the voice and will of God) from a far off land.

In type, God is speaking to both Isaac and Rebekah, and they both share with their parents, but in practicality it may work either way. Even if both individuals share with each other, it ought to be done among the confirmation of a multitude of counselors, beginning with the home. If both individuals are out of the home and on their own, there is still honor with parents, but on a different and equal level.

Here much discussion, in public among witnesses, takes place. As confirmation begins to take form, discussion of one another's home life, brothers, sisters, social background and upbringing takes place. This is not a time not to rush. It is a testing time to make sure it is the way God wants it. There is no jumping in too early and then asking others to confirm what has already been decided. That is not seeking counsel, that is simply seeking approval! If the marriage and wedding is assumed to already be decided, there is no real heart for confirmation or a fear of God in taking seriously the marriage covenant before God.

It is God's call and its confirmation that is most serious here. We must know if God is forming a new home! What joy! What a thrill we see in Rebekah's footsteps as she runs home to tell the news! All the waiting, serving and ministering in the team of her home could be coming to an end, and a new beginning, a new team, a beautiful team, could now be coming to birth through the timing and Spirit of God!

All confirmation is done in the open, before family members, and is still not done in secret, alone, or where temptation could blind the eyes and minds of those who are seeking God for a final confirmation. As one author put it, "our Christian forebears in their wisdom suggested that a courting couple should do nothing in private which they would not do in public".[16]

In a sense, this step is deciding whether it is time to leave father and mother (the first step in marriage.) It is important that one realizes that the closer you get to deciding upon God's call, the higher the fences need to be to protect your emotions for your own safety.

Betrothal - Engagement

> *"And they called Rebekah, and said unto her, Wilt thou go with this man? And she said, I will go."*
> - Genesis 24:58

---

[16] Barclay, Oliver R., *A Time to Embrace*, Inter-Varsity Press, Chicago, Illinois, 1964., page 17.

This is the step of true commitment. Let us ponder the meaning of betrothal:

> *"And I will betroth thee unto me for ever; yea, I will betroth thee unto me in righteousness, and in judgment, and in lovingkindness, and in mercies."* - Hosea 2:19

> *"Now the birth of Jesus was on this wise: When as his mother Mary was espoused to Joseph, before they came together, she was found with child of the Holy Ghost."* - Matthew 1:18

The word betroth from the Old Testament means *"to engage for matrimony."*[17] Here God is declaring his engagement to the nation of Israel through the allegory of Hosea and Gomar. Joseph and Mary were engaged when Mary became pregnant with Jesus by an act of the Sovereign power of God. The Greek word translated espouse means *"to give a souvenir or engagement present."*[18] Clearly we see that the concept of betrothal in Scripture is the same as engagement. In fact, it involves the dowry as well, signifying the origin of our word for wedding.[19]

A betrothal was a contract for marriage that was as solid as the marriage itself. In fact, one had to get a divorce in order to break it.[20] Thus, it is important to note that God waited until Joseph and Mary were betrothed and a solid commitment and covenant was made before having Mary conceive by the power of the Holy Spirit. Without a commitment from Joseph, Mary would have been rejected by Old Testament Law. Thus, Joseph, though tempted to "put her away," a phrase meaning divorce, he was told by God that it was the Lord's supernatural work that was occurring.

---

[17] Word #781 in Hebrew, *Strong's Concordance.*
[18] Word #3421 in Greek, *Strong's Concordance.*
[19] See Webster's 1828 Dictionary definition of "wed" meaning "wager" as well as "league."
[20] Rushdoony, *Institutes*, page 176.

This is precisely the point. Only when a clear commitment of engagement has taken place can emotions be released safely and securely within a relationship headed for marriage. What a joy, however, within this protection, to freely and voluntarily say YES. Now the Holy Spirit begins to join two individuals into the cleaving process. Here Rebekah rides, with the Holy Spirit (Eleazar) leading her, closer and closer to Isaac. Their emotions are now joined as well as their hearts. This is not a greater and greater physical involvement, but she is getting closer and closer to his heart.

A man and woman in this state should grow very close spiritually and socially. Thus, they begin to trust each other, and spend much time, not always alone, but also in company with others to protect themselves until the covenant is sealed on the wedding day. When one realizes that after you are married you will spend most of your time with others, it is important to do this in preparation as well. Prayer and devotions together, talk of all kinds of items and aspects of life are to take place at this stage of courtship.

In type this happened with Rebekah on her way "home" to Isaac. The servant must have told her many things about Isaac. In practical reality, it is the time spent together in social cleaving that one really begins to taste what life will be like together. The kind of dependency we often see during courtship and engagement of clinging and a public show of physical affection is usually the extension of the dating pattern and simply builds physically until the marriage, if the couple can wait that long.

This is very dangerous for the real cleaving and heart-to-heart knitting never takes place. It should be a time of close communication, but not dependency, and certainly not physical dependency. It is a time to see God step-by-step fulfilling His call and prophetic anointing over your life.

The Wedding and Reception

> *"And they blessed Rebekah, and said unto her, Thou art our sister, be thou the mother of thousands of*

> *millions, and let thy seed possess the gate of those*
> *which hate them."* - Genesis 24:60

This is the wedding. Notice her family, and we would also include the church, prophesying over her. They spoke words of exhortation, rehearsing the calling (which was the same as Isaac's) over her, reminding her that as she leaves her family, she is to fulfill God's call in possessing the gates of her enemies through her new home. What a joyous time of celebration!

This is a real wedding. Its purpose is not to show off the bride or the groom. It is a public time of celebration where confirmations and prophetic words of encouragement can forever remind one of the high calling of marriage and raising a family. The entire wedding ceremony can and should depict the process of courtship from beginning to end. It is a testimony that can be shouted from the housetops that God has kept His Word, and there are two individuals who have kept themselves pure until this moment!

> *"And Isaac brought her into his mother Sarah's tent,*
> *and took Rebekah, and she became his wife, and loved*
> *her.."* - Genesis 24:67

This is the final consummation of the wedding, becoming one flesh. Here we see that Isaac and Rebekah consummated God's call through physical union, or sexual intercourse. It was the external expression of what God had done internally. Total security and love could be released. Everything that had been kept and stored for this occasion is now released in love.

Thus, this process of courtship is unique, beautiful and has great meaning. May we, as a new generation, restore the true courting stage so that the foundations of many generations can be laid in the rock of the Lord's principles! Let us embrace His vision for our marriages!

Lesson Eight

LIFTING UP A STANDARD
Strengthening a Robbed Generation

*"So shall they fear the name of the Lord from the west,
and his glory from the rising of the sun. When the
enemy shall come in like a flood, the Spirit of the Lord
shall lift up a standard against him."* - Isaiah 59:19

A flood of impurity has been unleashed against the church in our
day. The decaying walls of many adult marriages are not holding it
back. Although there is a remnant of the adult generation that is
regaining its purity through the grace of God, and marriages are being
restored and/or rebuilt, the flood is still rising. The present teenage
generation is being destroyed through abortion. Those that survive are
being swept away by a flood tide of filth and sensual temptation that
promises to destroy future marriages before they even begin.

Today the divorce rate within the evangelical church often exceeds
the rate outside of the church, and as we noted in Lesson One, close to
90% of today's teenagers will lose their virginity by age 18!

The enemy seems to be winning. There is no proof of retreat from
within his ranks. But there is hope! A new teenage generation is
arising that is willing to restore the foundations of many generations.
They are not satisfied with gaining a little purity, they want to go God's
way whatever the cost! This new generation of teens will be made up
of youth who have kept their purity, as well as youth who have been set
free from their life of impurity. Together, as they work in teams, they
will restore a standard of purity to those around them. The contrast will
be so obvious that anyone who looks will see the difference.

The generation of teens who have kept their purity will bring
strength, stability, and an ability to disciple others in the way of the
Lord. Those set free from their past of impurity will bring a
gratefulness to God for their forgiveness that will attract even the most

vile offender of God's Laws. God has promised that in every generation He will lift up a standard (a flag, banner, or demonstration) against that flood tide of evil. I believe God's new generation of youth who keep themselves pure will be that standard and banner, drawing others in by the hundreds who will have experienced the devastation of a life of sin. We will see a generation that demonstrates what God has always intended in the earth!

What kind of a generation will be coming into the church in the next decade? A generation that knows little about virginity, much about extreme sinful behavior in men and women, and even less about Christ's purpose in bringing discipline into their life in order to curb sinful behavior and walk the way of the cross. The standards and principles we have been talking about here will be as foreign to them as a foreign language. Oh, that God would give us His compassion that we may reach them with God's love, forgiveness and grace!

How will God bring youth from both sinful and pure backgrounds and mold them together into the same army to be used of Him to destroy the gates of hell? Why should a generation seek to retain total purity if God can set one free from impurity anyway? Is it just for themselves and their own families? The answers to these questions are important. First, God has a greater purpose than to merely keep you pure for yourselves and your own family.

It takes strength to disciple. One must always minister out of strength. As one is kept pure by the Lord, he is prepared to minister in strength to those robbed of their virgin inheritance. Those kept pure by the grace of God will be able to disciple, teach, and restore those who come in by the grace of God from a past of impurity.

In God's Word there is the tender balance between the new and the old in the Kingdom (see Matthew 13:52). This is a precious balance between those who are old in the Lord, having held a standard of purity for years, and those that are new, filled with the grace from the Lord from a recent past of sin! Those who are kept from the impurity and stains of sin also need the demonstration of God's grace to those who have lost their inheritance of virginity. Some need to see those who are lost coming to Christ and receiving forgiveness for sins they have never thought of committing. Thus, those coming out of darkness into light in their teen years and beyond will demonstrate the ardent love, zeal, and gratefulness for a God Who will forgive them. They will supply something as well that is precious toward forming an army that is willing to rescue more and more teens in the days ahead!

We must embrace a vision of the calling of God to be examples and patterns for those who have never tasted of the Lord's goodness, laws or standards which protect us from such degradation and evil. We must see that the generation that keeps itself pure has a high calling to maintain the testimony of God in the earth for the sake of those He desires to bring out of bondage into glorious light. Though no one is better than anyone else, the greatest testimony is what God has kept you from, not merely from what you have been delivered.

When we see this, we will be able to see the purpose of restraining ourselves now for the days ahead. Preparation is always difficult if one does not keep the goal in mind. God wants us to be prepared to disciple the many thousands of teenagers who will be saved in the next decade in great need of healing, forgiveness, love, grace, and discipling in order to restore what the enemy has stolen. Our inheritance of virginity and purity will be an example to them.

Innocence Toward Evil

"... I would have you wise unto that which is good, and simple concerning evil. And the God of peace shall bruise Satan under your feet shortly. The grace of our Lord Jesus Christ be with you. Amen."
- Romans 16:19-20

Often when youth are kept pure they are somewhat embarrassed about how little they know experientially of evil. The common slang and experiences of the lost generation are almost foreign to them. Yet, we must realize God's purpose in all of this. We cannot be embarrassed about our lack of experience; we should be honored that God has kept us pure. Paul said here that he wished we all were wise about good, yet simple (unlearned, ignorant) about evil.

When one exposes himself to movies, television and other aspects of evil today, one's life, conscience, and heart are seared. It becomes more difficult to fight the devil. There is a hole in our armor. As we weaken more and more, but keep ourselves from overt acts or fantasies about sin, we become deceived. We think everything is fine, because we have not fully yielded to temptation, but have simply been planting the wrong seeds in our minds.

God has not called us to merely survive, however. He has called us to conquer. We are to be more than conquerors (Romans 8:37). We are not called to refrain from the acts of sin while indulging in the fantasies of sin! To simply keep oneself from evil for the sake of your own children, marriage and family is not enough. God needs to help us see His ultimate purposes.

Why would God want us to be innocent toward evil? Is it simply for our own sakes? No, not at all. It is for the ultimate goal of destroying the work of Satan and sin, and manifesting the Kingdom of God on earth! If you are kept pure, you will have both the power of God and the word of your testimony to overcome him. You will have crucified your own life (died to self) all during your youth for the time when you face Goliath. The stone of purity will do the rest. Based on what the blood of Christ has accomplished, your life will have been kept clean by the Word of God and His grace. Then, you will be able to deal with the devil properly and in God's way, defeating him by your testimony and lifestyle!

> *"And they overcame him (Satan) by the blood of the Lamb, and by the word of their testimony, and they loved not their lives unto the death."* - Revelation 12:11

Youth are Powerful Examples

> *"Let no man despise thy youth; but be thou an example of the believers, in word, in conversation, in charity, in spirit, in faith, in purity."* - I Timothy 4:12

124

Youth are destined to be powerful examples. God says that young men are known for their power over the devil (see 1st John 2:13). Youth are ordained with strength in order to overcome the adversary (Psalm 8:2). Youth are arrows, which will defeat the enemy in the gate as they join with adults (Psalm 127:5). Never underestimate, despise, put down, or belittle your role as an example and a standard bearer.

Examples in Word

Youth are to be examples in word. The way we talk, confess truth, and speak about the Lord, is powerful. What do we talk about? What are our favorite topics? Are we examples in the way God wants us to be? What we think about, we end up talking about, and the way we talk is usually the way we live (see James 3:2-6). After all, death and life are in the power of the tongue (Proverbs 18:21).

Examples of a Godly Lifestyle

Youth are to be examples in conversation, or lifestyle. The way you conduct your life has a tremendous influence upon others. Do you realize how many people are watching you? You probably are not aware of it. However, many people sit up and take notice when a young person is living differently than everyone else.

Examples of Godly Love

True love, agape love, that flows from one young person to another is like life and water to a parched land today. The only kind of love most teens know is one of lust for gain, not love for the benefit of another. Let us restore true love in our relationships, and as Jesus said, by our love we will convince people that He is truly Lord (John 13:35).

Examples of Faith

Youth are also examples in faith. Youth are willing to take risks, do things differently, and thus take steps of faith which adults at times

125

are not willing to take. The older one gets, the more like a fossil one is tempted to become! Thus, youth are needed to provide the zeal, heart, and faith that is necessary to launch out and fulfill God's vision for their generation! Their faith will go a long way in inspiring others!

Examples of Purity

Finally, youth are examples of purity. Yes, purity, the subject of this entire book. Our purity as teenagers and into single adulthood until we are married is a tremendous example to others. We need to realize how many people we can minister to through the example of our purity. Many younger children look up to those only a few years older than they. Our purity and testimony can actually be directing the next generation behind us!

Remember, by our example it is possible to overcome the enemy. It is possible to spread seed that will be planted along any route we take. Let's restore a generation of examples, standard bearers, so that the world will once again see that Jesus is real - and Lord of the nations.

Raising a Standard of Ethics

Webster defines ethics as *"the doctrines of morality or social manners."*[21] It is sorely lacking in our day and among the generations. We need to change this. By adopting some moral and mannerly ethics, we can go a long way toward setting an example worthy of emulation by the youth of our generation. Below are a set of brief guidelines that can help us lift up a standard of ethics as we minister to many that will be thirsting for the water of life. Ponder these practical tips on ministering to those who may not have had the inheritance that you are blessed to have received.

1.   We must maintain an attitude of ___love___ toward all people, regardless of their understanding or reception of holy standards. Love them just the way they are, though we cannot accept their sin as legitimate expressions of Godly living. They do not need to change in

---

[21] Webster's 1828 Dictionary, published by F.A.C.E.

order to receive love. Be interested in people and what they are interested in so that the love of Christ can draw them to Him.

2. Clearly distinguish between ***friendliness*** and worldly participation in your own mind. We can maintain a friendly atmosphere and acceptance of anyone, regardless of their background or life of sin, but we cannot compromise our own personal standards. Thus, there is no need to participate in sin (from the wrong kind of humor to sinful practices) but our attitude as to how we look at others will determine how well we are received as well.

3. Remember that the best way to share Jesus is through your ***testimony***. Some would argue that they don't have a testimony if they have not committed terrible sins in their past. However, the word of our testimony is what God has kept us from, not just what He has delivered us from. Our understanding of His precepts and standards, and why we believe them as well as their advantages, can be received when God's grace is evident in our lives.

4. Always maintain a positive and ***submissive*** attitude toward your parents and all those in authority. Nothing needs to be said, our actions will say it all. When others make fun of those in authority, we maintain the proper attitude. It is a solid testimony of honoring our parents and obeying God's commands.

5. Uphold the ***standards*** of team ministry in the presence of others at all times. The atmosphere alone will do more to soften hearts than a hundred sermons! Questions will begin to roll in as people behold your good works.

6. For the sake of our purity and the honoring of others, we must maintain the highest standards of ***dress*** at all times when ministering to others or among ourselves. The three key ingredients of a Biblical philosophy of dress are given below that help us form our standards:

"The woman shall not wear that which pertaineth unto a man, neither shall a man put on a woman's garment: for all that do so are an abomination unto the Lord thy God." (Deuteronomy 22:5) This principle is needed today. The clear **distinction** between masculinity and femininity needs to set by the believer in how he or she dresses. The blurring of all distinctions, from jewelry to clothing texture is an attack on the individuality of men's and women's roles.

"Doth not even nature itself teach you, that, if a man have long hair, it is a shame unto him? But if a woman have long hair, it is a glory to her; for her hair is given her for a covering." (I Corinthians 11:14-15) While we recognize that cultural variety exists around the globe and within nations, there is still a clear distinction in principle that must be made between men and women, including **hair style**. The hair is significant for it identifies us with a rebellious subculture or it separates us unto God in a way that is clear for all to see.

"In like manner also, that women adorn themselves in modest apparel, with shamefacedness and sobriety; not with braided hair, or gold, or pearls, or costly array; but (which becometh women professing godliness), with good works." (I Timothy 2:9-10; see also I Peter 3-4) Finally, it is important that we watch how we **_dress_** in general. Our dress should not bring attention to our bodies, but be graceful and modest, bringing attention to our character, as shown through our facial expressions and the way we conduct ourselves. Here we see that shamefacedness (embarrassment at immodesty) and sobriety (not loud, wild or bringing attention to ourselves) are the rules of ethics we ought to follow.

The "showboat" mentality of our age needs to be avoided. What we want people to remember is our good works, not our clothing! As we maintain these attitudes, we can be that blameless generation that lifts up a standard for all to see in the midst of a generation that has lost its bearings. Oh, that God would grant us favor as we continue to minister in His grace and wisdom!

What About Eunuchs?

"All men cannot receive this saying, save they to whom it is given. For there are some eunuchs, which were so born from their mother's womb; and there are some eunuchs, which were made eunuchs of men; and there be eunuchs, which have made themselves eunuchs for the kingdom of heaven's sake. He that is able to receive it, let him receive it." - Matthew 19:11-12

A eunuch is an unmarried person. As Jesus states here, some are that way physically at birth. In other words they are castrated, can never have children, and often never marry. Others through some manner in life or an accident, become this way physically. It certainly doesn't mean that one cannot marry simply because it would be impossible to give birth to children. However, Jesus states the fact that some accept their condition as a spiritual limitation to marry, giving themselves totally to the Lord and His service. Still others have no physical handicap at all, but voluntarily choose to be single for the sake of serving God in the kingdom way.

We must realize that there are young people who are called to be modem day eunuchs by choice. This is a noble call. As Jesus states, not all can receive it. Paul the Apostle stated the advantages of remaining single in I Corinthians 7. Among other things, he states that the advantages include:

(1) less trouble in the flesh, or in other words, more time can be given in devotion to the Lord because of less responsibility "in the flesh," or in supporting a home and ministering to a family (1st Corinthians 7:28).

(2) more concentrated devotion to the Lord, rather than concentrating on pleasing one's wife or husband (1st Corinthians 7:32-34.)

Each individual must be open to God's call to remain single. The principles in this book apply in a more serious way for those called to be single for life. Living in purity will be a lifelong calling so that one's example does not lend itself to distractions. Obviously, from Jesus' statement and Paul's, not many are called to this estate. However, we are primarily to serve the Kingdom and not ourselves, and so whatever His will is, we accept it.

Certainty if we keep ourselves pure, exercising self-restraint, it will be easier for us to accept this kind of call from God! The advantages to the married life are documented in the previous lessons. May God give grace to speak to each one of us in His perfect will as we serve Him in this life.

Shining in a Perverse Generation

"That you may be blameless and harmless, the sons of God, without rebuke, in the midst of a crooked and perverse nation, among whom you shine as lights in the world; holding forth the word of life; that I may rejoice in the day of Christ, that I have not run in vain, neither labored in vain. " - Philippians 2:15-16

We are called to shine! We are called to push back darkness. Let us examine some of the attitudes we must embrace in order to shine our testimony of purity into a land of impurity and darkness.

Blameless

The word blameless here means "irreproachable," or "without blame." When one lives his or her life above reproach, it means that the life is pure before God and man. This does not mean that we are without sin. It simply means that the enemy cannot get a hold on you because you are leaving cracks in the wall. Remember the broken down walls we spoke of earlier. Being blameless means you have built walls the enemy cannot scale. It is this kind of lifestyle that allows Jesus Christ to shine through you!

Harmless

Harmless means you are "innocent" and "unmixed" with evil. This is one of the strongest weapons against the enemy. Jesus stated that when we deal with the enemy we need to be *"wise as a serpent and harmless as a dove"* (Matthew 10:16). We are as wise as the enemy because we know his devices and are not fooled by his deceptions. We are harmless as a dove because we are not mixed up with evil and diluted in worldliness. What a combination! God is preparing each and every one of us to overcome the enemy in this way.

Sonship

We are not called to remain servants of the Lord. We are called to sonship. Whether you are male or female, in Christ we are all sons. A son knows what His Father is doing. A son has authority. A son understands that he is an heir to the throne of God (see Galatians 4:7). The Word of God speaks of many sons coming into glory all at once (Hebrews 2:10). What this means is that we are a part of a generation that wants to grow up in the Lord. We don't want to remain simply serving the Lord and emphasizing *receiving* from Him. We wish to *give* unto a lost generation in the power and grace that God gives us to care for others. Let us grow up into sonship and use the authority given to us by the Lord Jesus!

Without Rebuke

Do you always like being in trouble? I hope not. No one likes someone constantly correcting them and setting them straight. Well, it is about time that we all grew up so that we didn't need correction all the time. If we govern ourselves, we would not need as much external government. That is what being "without rebuke" really means. It means that we are dealing with our own nature and sin, taking it to the cross, and receiving forgiveness, so that we can live above our circumstances, over the enemy and over sin!

Holding Forth the Word of Life

In order to shine as lights, we must hold up, lift up, and bear the torch of God's Word for all to see. The Word of life is the Word of God, held high in our life and ministry. As we do this, we will see people drawn unto the Lord. It is important that we all gain a vision of what the Word of God can do in and through the life of people. Let us hold forth this word of life so that our lives are not lived in vain. May God help us as we work together to see His plan fulfilled!

A Final Word

When all is said and done, this life is but a vapor. Our lives, families and testimony will not last long when compared with eternity. Thus, our real inheritance lies in what we leave subsequent generations. What will you leave your children? What will you leave those younger than you are? What kind of memories will they have? Will they remember courage in the face of temptation, or selfish desires spent early in life with not much reserve later on. Oh that each one of us could embrace a vision of the kind of testimony David left for the generations that would follow him. He was, after all, a man "after God's own heart."

> *"For David, after he had served his own generation by the will of God, fell on sleep, and was laid unto his fathers..."* - Acts 13:36

General Bibliography

Barclay, Oliver R. *A Time To Embrace*; Inter-Varsity Press, 1964.

Bryant, Alton T. *The New Compact Bible Dictionary*; Zondervan Publishing House, 1967.

Gothard, Bill. *Establishing Biblical Standards of Courtship*, Commitment Booklet I; Life Purpose Network, Advanced Training Institute of America, Box One, Oak Brook, Illinois, 1990.

Graustein, Alan. *Teaching Biblical Principles Concerning Sexuality and Chastity*; Christian Fellowship School, 1988.

Lewis, C. S. *The Four Loves*; Harcourt Brace Jovanovich, Inc., 1960.

Marshall, Rev. Alfred. *The RSV Interlineal Greek-English New Testament;* Zondervan Publishing House, 1958.

Narramore, Clyde M. *Dating*; Zondervan Publishing House, 1961.

Rushdoony, Rousas John. *The Institutes of Biblical Law*; The Presbyterian and Reformed Publishing Company, 1973.

Slater, Rosalie J.; and Hall, Vema M. *Rudiments of America's Christian History and Government*; Foundation for American Christian Education, 1968.

Strong, James. *The Exhaustive Concordance of the Bible*; MacDonald Publishing Company.

Sprague, William B. *Letters in Practical Subjects to a Daughter*; reprinted by Sprinkle Publications, 1987.

Tomczak, Larry. *Let's Talk About Sex*; Vine Books, 1987.

THE HOLY BIBLE, King James Version; Thomas Nelson Publishers. All Scripture verses were from the King James Version unless otherwise specified. (NAS) - New American Standard Version; and (RSV) - Revised Standard Version.

Trobisch, Walter. *I Loved A Girl*, Harper & Row, Publishers, 1965.

Trobisch, Walter. *Please Help Me! Please Love Me!*, Inter-Varsity Press.

Vine, W. E. *An Expository Dictionary of New Testament Words*; Fleming H. Revell Company, 1966.

Webster, Noah. *An American Dictionary of The English Language*, 1828; republished in facsimile edition by the Foundation for American Christian Education, 1967.

Young, Robert. *Analytical Concordance to The Bible*; Wm. B. Eerdman's Publishing Company, 1964.

A Few Words About the Author
PAUL JEHLE

In the service of His Lord and Master, Paul Jehle wears a "coat of many different colors" - all purposed to fulfill Christ's Great Commission and Cultural Mandate.

Paul Jehle is Senior Pastor of The New Testament Church and founding principal of The New Testament Christian School of Plymouth, Massachusetts. Together with his wife, Charlene, and two children Jonathan and Shauna, he is founder and director of Heritage Institute Ministries (HIM) as well as serving as the Director of Education for the Plymouth Rock Foundation and its Christian Committees of Correspondence (CComCors).

In his role as pastor and overseer of both national and international outreach ministries, Paul Jehle conducts seminars and workshops on Christian education (teaching and administration), pastoral and youth leadership, and political statesmanship in the United States and many foreign nations.

A unique feature of the seminars are the student teams which often accompany Mr. Jehle on tour - living witnesses of the power of Christ in the lives of young persons and of the knowledge and abilities developed and honed through a Biblical world view applied to education.

The author of seven books, plus numerous booklets and widely-used taped teaching series, Paul's best known work is *Go Ye Therefore and Teach*. First published in 1982, it is now entering its third edition in two volumes and documents virtually every aspect of operating a Christian school from theology and philosophy to methodology and administration with sample guides in curriculum development throughout the grades. It is an invaluable guide for parents, administrators and teachers seeking to plan for, start and operate a Biblical School (one in which The Bible is the major textbook for each class and every subject). *Go Ye* is now used in Christian schools and homeschools across the United States and in more than 50 nations throughout the world. To order this or other works, simply call or write Heritage Institute Ministries or Plymouth Rock Foundation.

Dating vs. Courtship

A Few Words About
the Plymouth Rock Foundation

The Plymouth Rock Foundation has been described as "one of the premier educational institutions in the land today." John Beckett, founder and president of Intercessors for America, has said that the Foundation "is unexcelled in its ability to apply Biblical truth to contemporary issues."

Plymouth Rock is an uncompromising expositor of Biblical principles of self and civil government, economics and education. It believes Christ's perfect Law of Liberty is the one true lasting foundation for individual freedom and civil government.

Since 1970, the Foundation has sought to serve Jesus Christ by serving His people. Its mission is to help the members of its Pilgrim Family and Christian Committees of Correspondence (CComCors) to develop and apply a total Christian world and life view, thus to restore the Christian influence in the land. Its ministry incorporates research, education, publication, program development and local community service activities in the name of Jesus Christ.

The Foundation's materials focus on:
- Basic Biblical principles of government, education and economics;
- America's Christian history and Biblical foundations of the republic;
- Biblical principles concerning contemporary issues;

Throughout the nation - and, in fact, in many countries of the world, members and affiliates of Plymouth Rock's Christian Committees of Correspondence join together to pray, to study and apply God's word in all affairs and every area of life - and to serve Jesus Christ by serving others (Matt 25:31-46).

For further information on the Foundation's ministry and materials, and to learn how you can become involved in this Christ-centered, Bible-based work to restore the Christian influence in this nation, please write or call!

1120 Long Pond Road, Plymouth, Massachusetts 02360
1-800-210-1620

The followe ...*be leaders of men* **and nations!**